# CREATIVE SUBVERSION
The Liberal Arts and Human Educational Fulfilment

# CREATIVE SUBVERSION

## THE LIBERAL ARTS AND HUMAN EDUCATIONAL FULFILMENT

Edited by David Daintree

Connor Court Publishing

Connor Court Publishing Pty Ltd

PO Box 7257
Redland Bay QLD 4165
sales@connorcourt.com
www.connorcourt.com


ISBN: 978-1-925826-00-5

Cover design by Maria Giordano

Cover illustration: *Icarus*, H. Matisse, National Galleries of Scotland

Printed in Australia

# CONTENTS

# FOREWORD

*Archbishop Julian Porteous*

It is clear that Australia, along with most of the Western world, is experiencing a profound crisis of culture. I believe, as Paul VI argued, that this crisis has come about as a result of the split between Christian faith and the culture of the West. One of the ways in which we can start to address this crisis is through a return to the liberal arts approach in education. The idea of 'the liberal arts' can be traced back to classical antiquity, and perhaps is most embodied in the work of the ancient Greek philosophers. But I believe it achieved its fullest expression in its adoption by the Christian Church, in particular in terms of the classical theistic synthesis of faith and reason. This is an education that is open to both the truth of revelation and at the same time the working of unaided human reason seeking truth. It is through reason working on the basis of both revelation and human experience that we can, as Thomas Aquinas showed, move towards understanding the truth. In an age dominated by subjectivism, ideology and emotivism, which radically threatens human freedom, the development of an authentically liberal education provides a genuine sign of hope for the future of our society.

# INTRODUCTION

## David Daintree

This volume contains full texts of the papers presented at the third annual Colloquium of the Christopher Dawson Centre for Cultural Studies, in June 2017. The theme of the colloquium was Education, with a particular focus on liberal education as the proper basis not just for a career in the workforce but for a rich and fulfilling life.

Though we may reject as inadequate that materialistic Victorian belief in science-driven Progress, the fruit of the Enlightenment, it is undeniable that humankind is in progression. From a Christian perspective we are advancing from a Garden to the City of God. One of the indicators of the ineluctable movement in which we are all caught up is the mushrooming of the written record. Just 500 years ago libraries counted their books in the hundreds; now the size of the world's book stock is beyond reckoning. The effect of this growth on education has been cataclysmic, as the emphasis has necessarily shifted from gleaning facts to effectively culling them, from training memory to side-stepping it as a poor cousin to thinking in terms of abstraction and theory. In this state of unmanageable explosion of knowledge there is no going back to the simple monoculture of Christendom, nor is our world likely ever again to find complete agreement on a canon of Great Books that ought to be the common sustenance of educated men and women. The apparent hopelessness of this situation has given rise in our schools and universities, particularly in our arts faculties, to a kind of post-modern despair of ever finding objective truth, resulting in the spawning of a nebula of petty and unrelated subjects, many of which are driven by the ephemeral fancies of the day.

At a meeting with IBM executives at Yorktown Heights, New York, in January 1984 Dr Barry Jones (at that time Federal Minister for Science) asked, "What type of people are you looking for?" Their reply surprised him: "The same people we have always looked for – honours graduates in English or Philosophy who are good at playing chess."

If young people are taught well to communicate and to think, they can be trained, and re-trained, to do anything else. And to do it better than one who has had no basic training in humane skills. There is ample evidence to support this, and young people are themselves increasingly aware of the deficiencies in their own education. Anyone who has worked in an educational institution will have met intelligent students who realise that they have been short-changed.

The true conservative will not try to return to an imagined golden age, but will seek instead to identify those qualities in humanity that are universal, drill down into them with disciplined energy and extract the core material as the fundamental basis of all education for work and for life. For life: we have a higher calling than the beasts and every one of us needs more than an exclusively vocation-based training to satisfy our true needs and to reach our potential.

The Dawson Colloquia have become the high point of our year; the quality of our presenters is a testimony to their value and a guarantee (as far as anything can be in a changing world) of their continuance in the years to come.

I am grateful for the foresight and kindness of the Patron of the Centre, the Most Reverend Julian Porteous DD, Archbishop of Hobart, without whom the Centre would not have come into existence. Thanks are also due to the Principal, Council and Staff of Jane Franklin Hall for providing us once again with a most charming venue. I also acknowledge with deepest gratitude the support of the Committee and of the members of our International Advisory Board.

# CONTRIBUTORS

**Iain T. Benson**, PhD (Witwatersrand), JD (Windsor), MA (Cantab) is Professor of Law, School of Law, University of Notre Dame Australia, Sydney; Extraordinary Professor of Law, Department of Public Law, Faculty of Law, University of the Free State, Bloemfontein, South Africa; Visiting Professor, University of Western Ontario and a Senior Visiting Fellow, Massey College, University of Toronto (2015).

Currently Iain is Senior Fellow at the Chester Ronning Centre for the Study of Religion and Public Life, Alberta, Canada; Board and Executive Committee of the Global Centre for Pluralism, Ottawa, Canada; and an invited witness to the Australian Commonwealth Inquiry on Religion and Human Rights (2017).

He was retained by the Government of Canada to write on Religion and Public Policy (2008), one of the drafters of the *South African Charter of Religious Rights and Freedoms* (2010) and *rapporteur* on law and religion in Canada and South Africa to the Pontifical Academy for Social Sciences, Vatican (2014).

Dr Benson is the author of *Living Together with Disagreement: Pluralism, the Secular and the Fair Treatment of Beliefs by Law Today* (Ballan: Connor Court, 2012) and Iain T. Benson and Barry W. Bussey eds., *Religion, Liberty and the Jurisdictional Limits of the Law* (Toronto: LexisNexis, 2017, forthcoming). He is Editor of *Man Alive, The Ball and the Cross, The Flying Inn*, being Volume VII of the *Collected Works of G.K. Chesterton* (San Francisco: Ignatius Press, 2004).

He is also a published poet and musician (session penny-whistle and harmonica on various albums, most recently in South Africa January 2017). He divides his time between various countries and is the proud father of seven children.

**David Daintree** is a native of Sydney with a BA from the University of New England and an M Litt from Cambridge, completing his PhD in Tasmania. While his academic background is in Classics, he is primarily a medieval Latinist. Leaving school early, he worked in advertising and public relations before going on to university.

He has taught at Geelong Grammar School's Timbertop and was Senior Classics Master at St Peter's College, Adelaide. David later was Principal of Jane Franklin Hall, University of Tasmania, from 1984 to 2002, from 2002 to 2008, Rector of St John's College in the University of Sydney, then President of Campion College, Australia's only Liberal Arts college, from 2008 to 2012.

He has been a visiting professor at both the Universities of Siena and Venice, and a visiting fellow at St John's College, University of Manitoba, Canada. In 2013, at the request of Archbishop Julian Porteous, he became founding Director of the Christopher Dawson Centre for Cultural Studies.

David has led many educational tours overseas, mainly to Italy, but also to Central Asia and to the Oberammergau Passion Play. In 2017 he was made a Member of the Order of Australia in the Queen's Birthday Honours List.

He is married to Elizabeth and they have three grown-up children and four grandchildren. Their family home is in Colebrook, Tasmania.

**Kevin Donnelly** is one of Australia's leading education commentators and authors. He is currently Executive Director of the Education Standards Institute, a think-tank which he himself founded, and Senior Research Fellow at the Australian Catholic University. He was co–author, with Kenneth Wiltshire, of the Review of the Australian Curriculum.

Dr Donnelly taught English and Humanities for 18 years in Victorian government and non-government secondary schools and has also been a member of state and national curriculum bodies, including: the Victorian Education Department's Post Primary English Committee and Post Primary Taskforce, the Year 12 English Panel of Examiners, the Victorian Board of Studies and the federally funded Discovering Democracy Programme and inquiry into the Australian Certificate of Education.

Dr Donnelly has written extensively on contemporary developments in education for Australia's print media and is the author of *Why our schools are failing*, *Dumbing Down*, *Australia's Education Revolution* and *Educating your child: It's not Rocket Science*.

**James Gaston** is Assistant Professor of History at Franciscan University of Steubenville, Ohio. He received his MA from SUNY (State University of New York) Cortland and pursued doctoral studies at SUNY Buffalo with the renowned European intellectual historian, Dr Georg G. Iggers.

Professor Gaston is the Founding Director of The Humanities and Catholic Culture Program, the Franciscan University's flagship liberal arts program, inspired in part by the thought of the famed Catholic historian, Christopher Dawson. He has long been interested in the nature of the Catholic intellectual life; the unity, and history of the liberal arts; the thought of Christopher Dawson; the history and social structures of Christian culture; and the philosophy and history of geography.

His publications and papers include: *Catholic Culture: What is It and Why Should We Care About It?*; *Steel and the Upper Ohio Valley: A Study in Cultural and Regional Unity*; *The Sanctification of Work*; *Understanding Europe: Christopher Dawson's Vision of the Unity and History of Europe*; *The Political Thought of Fr Joseph Costanzo*; *The Catholic Intellectual and the Liberal Arts*; *The Making of the Catholic Mind: Christopher Dawson and the Spirit of the*

*Liberal Arts*; *Reflections on Christian Manhood*; *The Importance of the Geographic Perspective to the Catholic Social Sciences*; and *The Life and Thought of William F. Buckley, Jr*, among others.

Professor Gaston has been an associated with The Acton Institute, The Center of Christian Culture, The Heritage Foundation, NAPC*IS Council of Scholars, the Pennsylvania Geographical Society, Society for Christian Culture, and The Society of Catholic Social Scientists, among others. He is also a Senior Fellow at The Russell Kirk Center for Cultural Renewal.

Professor Gaston and his wife have eight children, many of whom still reside in Steubenville.

**Gary Johns** is a member of the Prime Minister's Community Business Partnership, a director of the Australian Institute for Progress, and president of Recognise What? Gary served in the House of Representatives from 1987-1996 and was Special Minister of State and Assistant Minister for Industrial Relations from 1993-1996. He served as an Associate Commissioner of the Commonwealth Productivity Commission 2002-2004.

Gary received the Centenary Medal and the 2002 Fulbright Professional Award in Australian-United States Alliance Studies, and served at Georgetown University Washington DC. He was Senior Fellow, Institute of Public Affairs, senior consultant, ACIL Tasman, Associate Professor, Australian Catholic University, and is Visiting Fellow at QUT Business School.

He holds a Doctor of Philosophy (Political Science) University of Queensland, Master of Arts (Geography) Monash University, and a Bachelor of Economics Monash University. Gary is also a columnist for *The Australian* and *The Spectator*. His recent books include: *Aboriginal Self-Determination* (2011), *Right Social Justice* (2012), *Really Dangerous Ideas* (2013), and *Recognise What?* (2014)

**Philippa Martyr** graduated from the University of Western Australia in 1994 with a PhD in the history of medicine. She taught for six years in what was then the Tasmanian School of Nursing in Launceston, before moving to the UK in 2001 to become a Visiting Scholar at Oxford Brookes University, Oxford, and a Visiting Research Fellow at the Wellcome Unit for the History of Medicine (then based at the University of East Anglia, Norwich). Dr Martyr then returned to Australia at the end of 2007, and spent the next nine years working for the WA Health Department as a researcher, project officer and clinical planner in mental health services.

Dr Martyr writes, publishes and speaks on a range of subjects, including her academic research specialities, religious issues, politics, higher education, film, literature, Australian historiography, and popular culture and psychology. She also publishes poetry, and very occasionally short fiction. Her work has appeared in (among other places): *Quadrant, AD2000, Australian Dictionary of Biography, Homiletic and Pastoral Review, First Things, Australasian Psychiatry*, the centre-right libertarian blog, Catallaxyfiles.com, and *Metascience*.

**Paul Morrissey** is President of Campion College, Australia's first Higher Education institution devoted to the study of the Liberal Arts. He holds a doctorate in Sacred Theology from the Catholic Institute of Sydney and a Licentiate in Sacred Theology from the Lateran in Rome. He is Adjunct Associate Professor of Theology in the School of Philosophy and Theology, University of Notre Dame, where he taught Theology for eight years.

**Julie Rimes** has a background in teaching which spans all sectors – State Department, Catholic and Independent schools, mainly in Tasmania but also the South Pacific and the UK. Her work has encompassed a variety of areas: teaching K-12, a Primary Principal for 15 years, curriculum adviser, and working extensively in VET within schools, TAFE and for an RTO. She has a strong research background and a body of published work to her credit.

From 2000 Julie was the Director of the Collegiate Institute in Hobart providing Vocational Education, Training and Professional Learning for the education sector. The Institute has developed relationships and partnerships with other providers to deliver a range of vocational learning experiences including Masters and Doctoral studies through Curtin University, where Julie worked as an Adjunct Senior Research Fellow, and the University of Tasmania where she is currently an Adjunct Associate Professor.

She is the Chairman of OakPossability, the largest disability provider in Tasmania and Chair of the Australian College of Educators national editorial committee. Her dedication to education and management has been recognised with a Fellow of the Australian College of Educators, Fellow of the Australian Council for Educational Leaders, Fellow of the Australian Institute of Company Directors, Honorary Life Membership of the Independent Primary School Heads of Australia and her inclusion in the Tasmanian Women's Roll of Honour.

**Karl Schmude** has combined a career in university librarianship and freelance writing with a formative role in the development of a liberal arts tertiary college. He has a BA from Sydney University, a Diploma in Librarianship from the University of NSW, and a Master of Letters from the University of New England (UNE).

Beginning at the NSW State Library in Sydney, he moved to Armidale, NSW, in 1970 where he worked in the University of New England Library for thirty years, serving as University Librarian from 1984 to 2000. He is a Founding Fellow of Australia's first liberal arts college, Campion College Australia, and serves as a Trustee of its governing body. From 2000 to 2015, he was Executive Director of the Campion Foundation. Most recently, he has been appointed as Chairman of the Board of St Albert's College, the Catholic residential college at the University of New England in Armidale.

Karl has published extensively on subjects associated with religion, history, literature and education. His feature articles and book reviews have appeared in Australian newspapers and journals as well as international periodicals in the USA, Canada, the UK and South America. He has written biographical booklets on G.K. Chesterton and Hilaire Belloc, and most recently Christopher Dawson (published by the Christopher Dawson Centre for Cultural Studies in Hobart). He is President of the Australian Chesterton Society and a member of the Editorial Board of the international journal, *The Chesterton Review*.

**Steven Schwartz** has an unusual blend of proven commercial skills combined with a strong background in education, health, governance and ethics. He is a prize winning researcher, teacher and public speaker, author of 13 books and over 300 articles as well as numerous radio and TV appearances.

He has a global track record in both executive and non-executive director roles as well as business management in higher education, research, medical and health management sectors. He was a former chair of the Fulbright Commission Board and a former Telstra Employer of the Year.

Steven has conceived and implemented academic and commercial capital developments including the Cochlear world headquarters and Macquarie University Hospital, and was named *Institutional Investor Magazine*'s Bond Personality of the Year. His special interests are higher education management, governance and leadership; health policy and management; ethics; education policy.

**John Simons** is a freelance writer, scholar and consultant who lives in Tasmania. He has worked in universities on every continent except Antarctica and most recently was Deputy Vice Chancellor (academic) at Macquarie University. Over nearly 40 years he has done every academic job from part-time lecturer to acting Vice Chancellor. He has written or edited some 20 books and numerous articles on a wide range of topics, but specialising in the history of animals, and is a published poet. He has recently completed his first novel.

# 1

# "Values Language": A Cuckoo's Egg or Useful Moral Framework?

## An Unresolved Problem in Moral and Ethics Education and in Catholic Thought

*Iain T. Benson*[1]

## Introduction

What I want to address here is a matter that is close to the core of Western moral education. It is an analysis of the use of the term values in relation to morality. Despite "the problem of values language" having been raised by many leading scholars, it still remains puzzlingly obscure. What is at issue is not simply whether

[1] The author thanks Dr David Daintree for the kind invitation to be a part of the Colloquium hosted by the Christopher Dawson Institute in Hobart, Tasmania at which a version of this paper was first presented in 2017 and to his colleagues Dr Angus Brook, Dr Steven Lovell-Jones, Dr Robert Anderson, Dr Robert Wagner, Profs. Renee Kohler-Ryan, Margo Somerville and Sandy Lynch, as well as in the School of Law at Notre Dame and the many students who have endured and contributed to numerous discussions about the "bankruptcy of values" over the last two years in legal philosophy, human rights and legal history classes; in particular Glynnis Nancarrow and Matthew French. He also thanks the members of the Small Circle Philosophical Discussion Group at its meetings in Basel and Frankfurt in 2014, 2015 and 2016 and, in particular, Profs Kristof Vanhoutte, Christo Lombaard and, in South Africa Prof. Shaun de Freitas. In Canada, Justices Peter Lauwers and Bradley Miller of the Ontario Court of Appeal. The opinions expressed are those of the author and not the faculties, schools, or institutes with which he is affiliated nor the people mentioned who may or may not endorse the criticisms of "values" in this paper.

the term "values" is purely subjective – based merely on personal assertions of the will (as some allege) or whether it serves a useful purpose in moral education and has shared moral meaning (as others allege) but, rather, whether it is wise to use the language of values at all in relation to teaching about morals and ethics when it has been demonstrated that it is harder to interpret virtues language subjectively and easier to interpret values language in that way. Where we are arguing for moral norms that are not subjective, then it follows that we are better off using the language of virtue than value. Much turns on the answer to this question.

This paper intends to marshal the arguments that indicate the nature of the problem and the significance for moral inquiry if the term "values" does introduce confusion over the subjectivity of moral claims as its opponents claim. Values language needs more attention than it has received from those who suggest that it serves a useful function in moral tradition or that it is consistent with the tradition of virtues education when many have denied these claims strenuously.

I also offer a three part taxonomy within which most (all?) writing on "values" and "virtues" may be classed. A condition of parallelism or confusion exists where the two terms and their differences are used interchangeably and, despite the plethora of scholarly criticism about the terminology of values, rarely brought into comparison. This usually happens because there is no recognition given to "the problem of values". This paper intends to challenge that status quo as unwise and suggests that "seeing through" the initial plausibility of "values" and substituting a richer frame – that of virtues – contributes to better transmission of traditions of moral and religious education. A third approach, where the two terms are analysed in terms of their differences and analysed contextually is the one taken in this paper.

One thing is certain: employing the language of values without addressing the growing body of scholars in various disciplines that have identified it as a language that corrodes the Western moral tradition is unhelpful. Simply asserting, for example, that "values are objective" or "values are universal" when there are strong arguments that this is not how most people understand "values", is not the most helpful approach. What is needed is critical analysis of the arguments that are opposed to the employment of values in ethics due to it being a vague term that introduces subjective confusion into moral claims. Engagement between the two sets of arguments is essential for clarity of what is a most confused and confusing area.

The alternative, simply saying, in effect, "move on folks, there is nothing here to see", simply promotes parallelism or confusion with the two different moral frameworks not engaging each other or simply merging without adequate delineation and explanation. If the claims of the critics of "values language" are correct, that it undercuts any respect for objective goods or intrinsic goodness or moral worth, then the debate is too important to ignore. It is also inappropriate to simply trot out that many have and continue to "use value language" in the face of such critiques if the users do not engage the identified problems.

**Part 1: A taxonomy of approaches to "values".**

I suggest the following categorisation of approaches to values (and virtues):

- **Parallelism:** This approach discusses "virtues" and "values" separately and does not bring them into conflict or conversation. It operates *as if* the two radically different approaches are part of the same tradition. This form may take a theoretical or institutional dimension. When, for example, a Roman Catholic institution, teaches "virtues" and "values" never addressing the "problem of values language" as I have set it out here, we see parallelism.

- **Confusion of "values" and "virtues"**: In this approach, values and virtues are discussed as if they are the same sorts of things. This category indicates confusion of the meanings but, as with Parallelism, does not analyse the difference in relation to the strikingly different results of virtues as understood as objective and values as subjective;

- **Engagement and analysis of both terms**: This approach aims at highlighting the "problem of values language" and seeing what each term "values" and "virtues" implies about moral tradition and the problems of subjectivism and relativism. This is the approach taken in this article and that it is argued should be pursued intentionally in Catholic and other ethical and moral education.

This article places itself, unlike many of the authors cited here who are in the first and second categories, in the third category above. The first part of this paper must now evaluate which approaches are most helpful and consistent with a long tradition of understanding shared virtues. The second part of this paper is an evaluation of an important book showing the second category above, the confusion of virtues and values.

**Opponents of "values" or those who criticise subjectivism but have not related this to "values".**

The term "values" is widely used and confusing – and this confusion has been only partially recognised within the Roman Catholic Church, which finds itself using this new language but in ways that do not, if the critics I shall review are correct, fit its metaphysics despite claims to the contrary.[2] The choice to use

---

[2] See: Philip Blosser "Values" in Michael L. Coulter, Stephen M. Kraso, Richard S. Myers and Joseph A Varacalli, eds., *Encyclopedia of Catholic Social Thought, Social Science and Social Policy* (Lanham: Scarecrow Press, 2007) 1110-1111; "The term values is used widely today not only in economics and philosophy but in psychology, the social sciences, the humanities and

the language of "values" to mean something that was believed to be inherently good, at a time when the term was rising to mean "personal choices" free from moral evaluation or its use within educational frameworks that sought to avoid ethics or morals, has led to wide-scale confusion about the meaning of "values".

How some understand the problem of "values language" is succinctly expressed by that wonderful quotation from Canadian philosopher George Grant when he said that: "values is an obscuring language for morality used when the idea of purpose has been destroyed."[3] I shall discuss this quotation in a greater context below. For our purposes at the outset, however, we might ask, what exactly is Grant saying here?

Grant was well aware that, as he put it:

> Everybody uses the word 'values' to describe our making of the world: capitalists and socialists, atheists and avowed believers, scientists and politicians. The word comes to us so platitudinously that we take it to belong to the way

ordinary discourse. Furthermore, it is used in a confusing variety of ways ... and stems largely from 19th and 20th century movements...one of the chief problems faced by value theorists is the challenge of giving an adequate account of the relationship between "values" and "facts," a legacy of the conventional distinction between "ought" and "is", and a problem underlined by Martin Heidegger's criticism of "values" in terms of "being"." The passage referred to by Blosser is most likely Martin Heidegger's scathing critique of "values language" in his "Essay on Humanism": "The bizarre effort to prove the objectivity of values does not know what it is doing [...] thinking in values is the greatest blasphemy imaginable against being" See: "Letter on Humanism" in *Basic Writings*, D.F. Krell (ed) ( San Francisco: Harper Collins, 1993) at 251. The relationship between phenomenology and "being" lie at the core of the confusions in this area but further exploration of them to the required depth is beyond the scope of this article. I hope to pursue this and other related notions, in later work.

[3] David Cayley, *George Grant in Conversation* (Toronto: Anansi, 1995) 120-122. See the fuller quotation in the text accompanying footnote #13 below.

things are. It is forgotten that before Nietzsche and his immediate predecessors, men did not think about their actions in that language. They did not think that they made the world valuable, but that they participated in its goodness.[4]

Grant is pointing out, first, that this language of values obscures morality. On this reading, "values" is a false sort of moral language – a trickster, one that offers what it does not and cannot deliver. Second he points out that the language is widespread. This language, "my values, your values", is generally taken to be a moral language and some are quite content with the subjective dimension of it whilst others are not and still others claim, against the trend of subjectivism, that "values" are necessarily objectively moral when the first group would strongly reject this claim.

Due to the centrality of "values" in discussions around schooling and due to its centrality in what passes for contemporary education but is actually more *schooling* than education, since little of tradition is explored, this term and its framework needs to be examined closely and thought about much more than it is at the moment. This claim, that "values language" actually cuts moral education off at the core, will be a surprise to some who think it is an acceptable moral language and even employ it in their work. As Grant and others noted, this "language of values" is used by practically everyone these days, including those who occupy traditions much older than this new period of "values language" – yet earlier traditions spoke of "virtues" relating to the "good" entailed in the framework of virtues itself not of "values" that are merely personal choices or where the word is almost entirely used in that way – "*my* values/ your values". Virtues entail and always have, a shared moral tradition, "values" do not despite some simply asserting that

---

[4] George Grant, *Time as History* (Toronto: Canadian Broadcasting Corporation, 1969) 44-45.

they do.[5] It is not possible to speak of a purely personal "virtue" yet

[5] See Kenneth L. Schmitz, *At the Centre of the Human Drama: The Philo-sophical Anthropology of Karol Wojtyła/ Pope John Paul II* (Washington DC: Catholic University of America Press, 1993) 81-83. In this study of the writings of Karol Wojtyła, who became John Paul II, the author explicates the approach to "values" as follows: "... at the centre of the personal project of each human being is the individual's conscience agency ... *Feelings in themselves do not determine values or our knowledge of them* – the reference is to the author's ongoing critique of Scheler – though they frequently accompany our relation to them: "The fusion of sensitivity with truthfulness is the necessary condition of the experience of values" (citing *The Acting Person* 233). Later Schmitz notes that "In this acknowledgement of the role of metaphysics (in *The Acting Person* 186)...we also recognise the objective order of goods as part of the real order of beings." Finally, " *Values are not subjective and are not constituted by subjectiveness* . Indeed if I do not overstate the author's realism on this point, while all the subjective elements that partially constitute the human person may come into play in action, *values do not differ in reality from goods; they are those same goods insofar as they offer to the person the genuine possibility of becoming more effectively human. It is here that the metaphysics of the good joins the phenomenology of value within human and personal act.*" 81-83 (emphasis added); So much for the *goal* of John Paul II's framework. Sadly once one reviews the breadth of writings on "values" across philosophical theorists, and where this has led in relation to Catholic use of "values" in confusing ways, it is difficult to avoid the stark conclusion that merely affirming that "values" are "objective" and not relative or based on feelings as Wojtyła attempted to do, fails when one regards how the language is used generally. The attempt failed because such a construction of "values" as *necessarily moral or oriented to the good*, seems to be precisely the opposite construction of "values" to that which the non-phenomenological philosophers have identified. Had Wojtyła used the entailed phrase "*choice for good*" and "*choosing the good*" both of which keep the actor and the good together, for the human act in relation to the objective category chosen, rather than the unentailed subjectivist and relativist term "values" (which by then had been framed by Nietzsche as par excellence the language of the will to power) his writing in this area would have been clearer, better for pedagogy and far less confusing for the Catholic tradition as we shall see when we look further into current Catholic teaching and commentary in this area. See: Karol Wojtyła (Andrzej Potocki transl.) *The Acting Person* (Dordrecht: D. Reidel Publishing Co., 1979) "the important thing in human striving is its truthfulness – the striving must correspond to the value of its object" (171). That "values" throughout this central work

values are precisely personal with the hidden secondary dimension that, having asserted ones' values one should not "push them on someone else."

Values language, however, according to analysts of the third category, is the lexical equivalent of the cuckoo's egg.[6] Having been laid in our nest of language sometime alongside other eggs that are used to drive religion and its moral languages to the margins of culture – here one might mention the terms "secularism" and "secular" (in its new use both around the mid 19th Century) and more recently additional nest-mates such as "progressive", "equality", and most recently "inclusion" as additional terms to note for their fledgling killing capacities, the language acts to obscure moral discourse.

All these terms, so goes the reasoning, have muscled out the other fledglings, the traditional moral fledglings, such as "virtues" from the nest and these have, in effect, fallen to the ground where they have largely expired. Most people have not even noticed the substitution or what "values" do not offer to a moral tradition once framed within "virtues".

---

are assumed to be correlated to "truth" marks this usage out as being in stark contradiction to how "values" are used generally. The same confusing use of "values" alongside "virtues" also occurs in Karol Wojtyla (transl. H.T. Willett) *Love and Responsibility* (San Francisco: Ignatius Press, 1993) 166-169; 196-198. Other terms would have been less ambiguous, more helpful and less confusing. This essential problem is widespread in Roman Catholic authors including examples that may be found in the works of Jacques Maritain, Hans Urs von Balthasar, Bernard Lonergan and Dietrich von Hildebrand. For an attempt to defend John Paul II's use of "values" without attending to the problem of the term itself see: Thomas D. Williams, "Values, virtues and John Paul II", *First Things*, April 1997.

[6] The cuckoo bird has the practice of laying its eggs in the nests of other birds. The eggs are then tended by the host bird which, unaware that it is hatching cuckoo fledglings, is also unaware that the hatchlings will, at the earliest opportunity, push the other fledglings out of the nest to their deaths. What looked like the host's own eggs were in fact a mortal threat to its own continuance. The metaphor's application to "values language" in the nest of "virtues" is, I hope, clear.

Many did notice the remarkable shift from the idea of pursuing the good to simply, more or less, asserting one's own feelings about things. Though many have commented on the problem of subjectivism, fewer have traced that a major element in this subjectivising has been, precisely, the employment of "values" in the subjective turn.

C.S. Lewis, for example, in his essay "the Poison of Subjectivism" and book *The Abolition of Man* noticed the turn to the subjective but nowhere commented on the problem being located in or exacerbated by "values language" itself.[7] On the

---

[7] C.S. Lewis, "The Poison of Subjectivism" (1943), in Walter Hooper ed. *Christian Reflections* (Grand Rapids: Eerdmans, 1967) 81; *The Abolition of Man* (New York: Macmillan, 1947). In the latter, Lewis speaks of "traditional values", "real values" and "objective values" in all cases suggesting that a theory of "objective value" is exigent. He writes that, "[a]dogmatic belief in objective value is necessary to the very idea of a rule which is not tyranny or an obedience which is not slavery" (44). Lewis, in common with many writers cited elsewhere in this chapter, appears unaware of how the term "values" *itself* exemplified and embodied the subjective relativism he rejected and that merely attaching the terms "traditional", "real" "transcendent" or "objective" does not overcome the difficulty. John Paul II, chose the term "universal values" as a claim (unhelpful and confusing) that "values" were necessarily sharing in objective goodness – against the trend of some of the other writers here who understood that "values" cannot be saved from the subjective trap by simply appending them to a noun – collective or otherwise. Lewis' blind  spot here is interesting and widely shared by other authors who sought to employ "values" of one sort ("objective", "transcendent", "traditional"" etc.) as if they were a counter to "subjective values". This failed attempt to make "subjective values" do the work of an objective moral framework, a failure which forms the core of the current article, has had profound consequences for morals and ethics in the contemporary age yet been too rarely noted. This despite the fact that leading theorists of "value" have noted "… the concepts of intrinsic goodness and badness cannot be defined adequately in terms of the concepts of evaluation and valuing" see: Ramon M. Lemos, *The Nature of Value: Axiological Investigations* (Gainsville: University Press of Florida, 1995) 63. This article is part of an intended suite of writings that will examine the depredations of "values" particularly on the disciplines of theology, philosophy, education, politics and law and wider society in general.

other hand, Allan Bloom, whose *The Closing of the American Mind*[8] made such an impact when it appeared, in that work and his earlier literal translation of *The Republic of Plato* noted both the prevalence and radically subjective and relativising nature of the language of "values" and its role in bolstering a related phenomenon, that of the explosion of "feelings" rather than "reason" in contemporary formulations, particularly by the young.[9] Alasdair MacIntyre, in his justly celebrated *After Virtue*, noticed, the emotional (emotivism) and the turn to the subjective and the relative,[10] as did John Rist in his *Real Ethics*[11] but not as powerfully as others I shall mention in this paper. Recently Pierre Manent's *Secularism in Europe*[12] has made the point clearly as well that "Republican values" did not and could not generate the virtues of the Republic.

Again, Canadian philosopher George Grant has addressed, in various ways, the shallowness or bankruptcy of "values" and commented on the origins of that language, noting that:

> It seems to me that Nietzsche is clearly saying there are no inherent purposes in the world. What people had previously meant by "good" was what anything was fitted for: a horse was good if it could run fast or pull. Good was what we were fitted for, or what we *are* fitted for. That implies purpose. It's good for human beings to breathe;

---

[8] Allan Bloom, "Preface" to *The Republic of Plato* (New York: Basic Books, 1968) ii-xxii.

[9] Allan Bloom, *The Closing of the American Mind* (New York: Simon and Schuster, 1987) 194-216.

[10] Alasdair MacIntyre, *After Virtue: A Study in Moral Theory* (Notre Dame: Notre Dame Univ. Press, 2nd ed. 1984) 11-35.

[11] John Rist, *Real Ethics: Reconsidering the Foundations of Morality* (Cambridge: Cambridge University Press, 2002).

[12] Pierre Manent (transl. Ralph C. Hancock) *Beyond Radical Secularism* (South Bend: St Augustine's Press, 2016) 85.

that was *good*. This was the old language. Nietzsche no longer believes that there are these purposes; the purposes have been destroyed. He wants a new language to express how we decide what we should do, and therefore he substitutes for the language of good what we are fitted for, the language of value ... No one can tell me what a value is. It seems to me an obscuring language for morality once the idea of purpose has been destroyed ... Everyone talks about values, night and day, when they're trying to make pious, secular sermons; and yet it comes from the greatest enemy of all this, Nietzsche. The language of value is above all the language of Nietzsche. It is what is left once you have eliminated the idea that there are purposes that intrinsically belong to being, like breathing ... The idea of values disguises existentialism within an apparent platitude. It prevents people from thinking about matters they should be thinking about.[13]

Grant realised, in addition, that this language was used, as we have seen, by religious adherents as well as others but in a manner that undercut the worldview religions actually develop. He wrote:

What is comic about the present use of "values", and the distinction of them from "facts", is not that that it is employed by modern men who know what is entailed in so doing: but that it is also used by "religious" believers who are unaware that in its employment they are contradicting the very possibility of the reverence they believe they are espousing in its use.[14]

---

[13] David Cayley, *George Grant in Conversation* (Toronto: Anansi, 1985) 120-122.

[14] Joseph Power "Grant's Critique of Values Language" in *George Grant in Process*, Larry Schmidt ed. (Toronto: Anansi, 1978) 90 at 94 "Grant is saying, as forcefully as he can that "values" is not what has been meant by "the good".

As Allan Bloom puts it, succinctly, "since values are not rational and not grounded in the natures of those subject to them, they must be imposed. They must defeat opposing values. Rational persuasion cannot make them believed, so struggle is necessary ... Commitment is the moral virtue because it indicates the seriousness of the agent."[15]

Philosopher Edward Andrew has noted that "there has been only partial awareness in the academy that the language of values entails that nothing is intrinsically good and no one is intrinsically worthy".[16]

Gertrude Himmelfarb, the noted historian, has pointed out that values "... because it seemed so familiar and unthreatening, ...was all the more effective, for it was absorbed unconsciously and without resistance by the ethos of modern society as it was absorbed into the vocabulary". The difficulty, however, was that "values ... brought with it the assumptions that all moral ideas are subjective and relative, that they are mere customs and conventions, that they have a purely instrumental, utilitarian purpose, and that they are peculiar to specific individuals and societies ... the word "virtue" carried with it a sense of gravity and authority, as "values" does not."[17]

---

[15] Allan Bloom, *The Closing of the American Mind* (New York: Simon and Schuster, 1987) 201.

[16] Edward Andrews, *The Geneology of Values: The Aesthetic Economy of Nietzsche and Proust* (Lanham: Rowman & Littlefield, 1995) 170. This insight shows the stark difference between these criticisms and the claims of "values" supporters such as Bernard Lonergan and John Paul II who claim exactly the opposite.

[17] Gertrude Himmelfarb, *The De-moralization of Society: From Victorian Virtues to Modern Values*, (New York: Alfred A. Knopf, 1995) 11. An irony of Himmelfarb's analysis and its application directly to the book discussed in Part 2 of this article, is the observation she makes that in "a thoroughly relativistic climate such as our own, even "values" may be seen as a retreat from relativism and a reassertion of moral principles" (16). In this setting, even "values" can become "a code word" for "virtues". A move such as this is precisely what one sees in the book examined in part 2 below and makes up the second category in the three part taxonomy I have suggested – namely, *confusion*.

For Princeton's Jeffrey Stout, the language of values is, in fact, an aspect of a confusion fitting a post-Babel theological framework: "… the primary language in which we understand ourselves is shot through with individualism and is therefore ill-suited for public discourse about the common good or for shaping meaningful lives."[18]

In his important essay from 1946, "Politics and the English Language", George Orwell identified the role that "meaningless words" play in relation to politics and identified "values" as one of a list of such words. He says that thought can corrupt language and language can, in turn, corrupt thought. A bad usage can spread by tradition and imitation even among people who should and do know better."[19] In relation to the virtue of justice and the tradition of the virtues, is not recourse to "values" exactly the sort of corruption Orwell was getting at? Authoritarianism, subjectivism and relativism are checked not by vagueness but by moral clarity.

The economist and historian Ludwig von Mises has summed up the difference between statements about truth and falsity and "judgements of value". He writes:

> Presuppositions asserting existence (affirmative existential propositions) or nonexistence (negative existential propositions) are descriptive. They assert something about the state of the whole universe or of parts of the universe. With regard to questions of truth and falsity they are significant. They must not be confounded with judgments of value.

---

[18] Jeffrey Stout, *Ethics After Babel: The Languages of Morals and Their Discontents* (Cambridge: James Clarke & Co., 1990) 191.

[19] George Orwell, *The Collected Essays, Journalism and Letters,* Sonia Orwell and Ian Angus (eds) Vol VI, 1945-1950 (London: Penguin) 156-170 at 161-162.

Judgements of value are voluntaristic. They express feelings, tastes, or preferences of the individual who utters them. With regard to them there cannot be any question of truth and falsity. They are ultimate and not subject to any proof or evidence ....

It is thus obvious that any scientific treatment of the problems of value judgements must take into full account the fact that these judgments are subjective and changing. Science seeks to know what is, and to formulate existential propositions describing this universe as it is. With regard to judgments of value it cannot assert more than that they are uttered by some people and inquire what the effects of the action guided by them must be. Any step beyond these limits is tantamount to substituting a personal judgment of value for knowledge of reality. Science and our organised body of knowledge teach what is, not what ought to be.[20]

For Eric Voegelin, clarity about the attempt to make political science and social sciences in general "objective" required a "methodologically rigorous exclusion of all 'value-judgements'." In order to understand this, Voegelin notes:

... the terms "value-judgement" and "value free" science were not part of the philosophical vocabulary before the second half of the 19th century. The notion of a "value-judgment (*Werturteil*) is meaningless in itself; it gains its meaning from a situation in which it is opposed to judgments concerning facts (*Tatsachenurteile*). And this situation was created through the positivistic conceit that only propositions concerning facts of the phenomenal world were "objective" while judgments concerning the right order of soul and society were "subjective."

---

[20] Ludwig von Mises, *Theory and History: An Interpretation of Social and Economic Evolution* (Westport: Arlington House, 1969) 19, 35-36.

Only propositions of the first type would be considered "scientific", while propositions of the second type expressed personal preferences and decisions, incapable of critical verification and therefore devoid of objective validity.[21]

Moreover, Voegelin comments on the effects of this move by concluding that, " In so far as under the concept of value-judgments was subsumed the whole body of classic and Christian metaphysics, and especially of philosophical anthropology, *the attack could result in nothing less than a confession that a science of human and social order did not exist.*"[22]

The analysis here is not, however, all one way with "values" being unrelated to human good discussed in an objective sense. In a current closer to that of Karol Woytjla (whom I shall discuss below), Bernard Lonergan asserts that values are transcendental and essential to the human good. For him, "[j]udgements of value differ in content but not in structure from judgements of fact ... The judgment of value, then, is itself a reality in the moral order. By it the subject moves beyond pure and simple knowing. By it the subject is constituting himself as proximately capable of moral self-transcendence, of benevolence, of true loving."[23] For Lonergan, unlike many who are critical of "values language", values are necessarily related to the good. He does not see the subjectivity of values in the negative manner indicated by other authors. He notes as follows:

---

[21] Eric Voegelin, *The New Science of Politics: An Introduction* (Chicago: Chicago University Press, 1952, 1987) 11.

[22] Ibid. 12 (emphasis added).

[23] Bernard J.F. Lonergan, *Method in Theology* (Toronto: University of Toronto Press, 1971) 37. "In the measure that the summit is reached, then the supreme value is God, and other values are God's expression of his love in the world, in its aspirations, and in its goal. In the measure that one's love of God is complete, then values are whatever one loves, and evils are whatever one hates ..." (39).

It is by the transcendental notion of value and its expression
in a good and uneasy conscience that man can develop
morally. But a rounded moral judgment is ever the work of
a fully developed, self-transcending subject or, as Aristotle
would put it, of a virtuous man.[24]

The relationship between judgments of objective value and
beliefs is important here and Lonergan suggests something akin
to the problem others, but not he, perceive as inherent in "values
language" itself. He writes:

> For convictions and commitments rest on judgments of
> fact and judgments of value. Such judgments, in turn,
> rest largely on beliefs. Few, indeed, are the people that,
> pressed on almost any point, must not shortly have
> recourse to what they have believed. Now such recourse
> can be efficacious only when believers present a solid
> front, only when intellectual, moral, and religious skeptics
> are a small, and, as yet, uninfluential minority. But their
> numbers can increase, their influence can mount, their
> voices can take over the book market, the educational
> system, the mass media. Then believing begins to work
> not for but against intellectual, moral and religious self-
> transcendence. What had been an uphill but universally
> respected course collapses into the peculiarity of an
> outdated minority.[25]

---

[24] Ibid., 41. This quotation is accompanied by a tantalising footnote in which
Lonergan writes as follows: "While Aristotle spoke not of values but of virtues, still his account of virtue presupposes the existence of virtuous men, as
*my account of value presupposes the existence of self-transcending subjects*"
(f.n.#23, 41 emphasis added).

[25] Ibid. 244. See also, Michael Vertin, "Judgments of Value, For the Later
Lonergan" *Method: Journal of Lonergan Studies* 13 (1995) 221-248 tracing
how for Lonergan "…unrestricted love transforms ordinary value judgments
into religious value judgements" (248).

So for Lonergan the beliefs that undergird the "true loving" that frame his notion of proper values can, in fact are likely to, decrease along with a decrease in belief itself. Here, Lonergan and others who assume that "values" are necessarily objective, also observe that these uses can, under the influence of scepticism, collapse leaving the prior notions little but a form of eccentricity – the general use being one in which sceptical beliefs frame an approach to "value" that is anything but the sort of self-transcendence measured against the good that Lonergan began by advocating. We see here how a Catholic philosopher noted for the rigour of his analysis claims that values are related to transcendent notions of good but also that such relations depend upon faith that may vanish leaving "values" themselves cut off from the belief that gives them objective meaning. This being the case, the wisdom of using values in an age of scepticism is questionable even where "values" were seen as necessarily objective.

Having canvassed the authors listed above, from such a wide variety of disciplines, we should ask this question: knowing what we now know of "values language" is it wise now (if it ever was) to use "values language" in courses teaching ethics and morals and, *a fortiori*, in Catholic Institutions the moral traditions of which were framed, not in relation to "values" but to "virtues"?[26] I would like

---

[26] The "Objects" of the University of Notre Dame Australia, set out in part on a brass plaque in each classroom under a plain wooden cross proclaim that the University seeks to uphold, inter alia, university education within a context of "Catholic faith and values." The *Compendium of the Social Doctrine of the Church* (Washington D.C.: United States Conference of Catholic Bishops and the Pontifical Council for Justice and Peace, 2009) is discussed further below at footnote #38. This strange grouping of virtues alongside concepts such as "freedom" and suggestion that these "social values" emerge somehow from the dignity of the person, makes a dog's breakfast of the traditional virtues of the Church (discussed in earlier sections of the *Compendium* and in the *Catechism* of the Church itself). One almost has the sense that the compilers of the *Compendium* needed to account for appearance of the

to share a personal experience here as it is relevant to give further context to this important question.

A few years ago, having argued the case against "values" in an intervention at a meeting of the Pontifical Academy for Social Sciences at the Vatican where I had been invited as a Rapporteur on Law and Religion to a Session on Religious Diversity,[27] its then President, the wonderful Mary Anne Glendon from Harvard Law School, asked, "you have made a compelling argument against "values" but what are we supposed to do, we've been using this language in the Church for decades?". That the academicians present offered no defence of the language *per se* is telling. In response to her somewhat plaintive question, what came to mind on that occasion was something G.K. Chesterton, who did not write about "values" at all, once wrote somewhere: when one realises that one is on the wrong road the wisest thing to do is to get back on the correct one.

Where the Church has attempted to clarify the relationship between principles and "social values" the result is an astonishing mix of notions taken from the framework of "virtues" with concepts that are not properly virtues or are other ideas entirely. It is as if the attempt to provide clarity just further deepens the confusion.

In his literal translation of Plato's *Republic,* in fact, Allan Bloom notes in the "Preface" that some translations of Plato have

---

category of "values" in various Church documents but didn't know precisely how to join them together with principles and virtues. The result is, to say the least, confusing and its effect on the ancient tradition of virtue and claims of objective good in relation to purpose unlikely to be salutary.

[27] Plenary Session 29 April -3 May 2011, Mary Ann Glendon, Hans F. Zacher (eds) *Universal Rights in a World of Diversity: the Case of Religious Freedom* (Vatican City: Pontificiae Academiae Scientiarum Socialium, 2012, Acta 17); the Intervention on "Values" as is common with interventions, was not part of the published volume.

translated "the good" as "values" and that the translators seem not to be aware that for contemporaries "values" is the language of preference and it is assumed that these are bound to be largely if not purely personal. The "values" world, call it that, is one in which two axioms predominate: 1) "You have your values and I have mine" (it is not assumed at all that these will overlap or that there is a shared and necessary moral goal in mind); and 2) "Don't force your values on me" (this flows from the first point and sets the stage for the personalising and relativism of whatever is being discussed). Bloom knew what, sadly, Karol Wojtyła and many others have ignored, dismissed as unimportant, or, less frequently, denied.

**Part 2: Use of "values language" as a language: a review of *Giving Voice to Values***

*Giving Voice to Values* ("GVV") by Mary Gentiles[28] is a book that is at the centre of a project and the project takes its name from the book.[29] The book is used quite widely at the Catholic University at

---

[28] *Giving Voice to Values: How to Speak Your Mind When You Know What's Right* (New Haven: Yale, 2010) ("GVV"). I thank Dr Sandy Lynch for bringing this book to my attention and for giving me and others the opportunity to meet and engage with its author at an academic symposium held at the University of Notre Dame Australia, Sydney, in September 2016. The critique of the GVV book and its project which follows was presented to the author – without, to date, any academic response from her or those who support her approach *in relation to the problem of values language discussed in this paper*. Quoting others in support of this book without engaging "the problem of values language" is not an adequate academic response to the problems identified.

[29] In an online interview with Dr Gentile by Dr Mark Jenner, the GVV project is claimed by Dr Gentile to be "an innovative approach to values-driven leadership development.....what I've found [states Dr Gentile] … is that people often did know more often what was the right thing to do but they didn't know how to do it effectively....it asks and answers a different question when it comes to values and leadership. Instead of asking what is the right thing to do in any particular situation, which, of course is an important and good question, what GVV does is ask once you know what is right how can you get

which I teach and the author came to give a number of presentations relating to her project in September of 2016, at which time most of this criticism was presented to her. So clearly does this book exemplify the support of "values", within the framework others have described as subjectivist and confused, that it will serve as a good example as an approach to "values" that some apparently deem acceptable and useful pedagogically but I describe as the confused second category above.

The book begins with a critique of existing ethics programs and the statement that "what we really need now is preparation and practice for action, and not just any action but a particular kind of hard, often risky, intricate values-based action" (xi). The project of "Giving Voice to Values" has a mission, a long list of jacket blurbs using words like "courage" and "ethics" and sets out to address the need to "improve corporate culture". The book has won awards for "business ethics" and has a prestigious publisher, it is clearly popular and has spawned a website, curriculum methodology and peer review guides. What does the author believe and how useful is this project? To that I shall now turn.

---

it done effectively, what do you need to do in what sequence and what would the push back be....": <http:youtu.be/9gKie7qSimc> (last accessed March 20, 2018). The entire project assumes the validity of moral positions without teaching them and without challenging the subjectivism of the "values frame-work" itself. The project carries on as if the criticisms of "values" simply do not exist and as if whatever any particular person's conception of "right" is valid. This is a project supported by Unilever and widely supported by large corporations and many are the business leaders who have found the approach of GVV powerful and helpful. The focus is on "empowerment" of the individual will – yet without an articulation of an ethical or moral frame-work itself. One wonders how its author or those employing this framework could have imagined that it would stand up to another sort of "new values" – those required as exercises of mere will in the "transvaluation of all values" that should undergird Nihilism as explained by Friederich Nietzsche, in his "Preface (Nov. 1887-March 1888)" in *The Will to Power* , (transl. Walter Kaufmann and R. J. Hollingdale), Walter Kaufmann (ed) (New York: Vintage Books, 1968) 3-4.

## The claims of GVV

The first claim of the book and the project is that it will help people learn and be "empowered" to "speak your mind when you know what is right", in fact this is the book's sub-title. So, at least in relation to intention, the book seeks a connection between the person, the dilemma and the idea of "what's right" and seeks to improve the role of individual employees and corporate culture in so doing. GVV, however, is not a moral project if by "moral" we mean one that employs shared moral meanings in relation to its end.

What is key here is the justification for the project. The book sees itself as part of a movement for "values-based action" (xi) and wishes to "transform the foundational assumptions of the teaching of practical principled management" so as to "equip future business leaders to know what is right and how to make it happen" (xvii). And what is this "right" since the moral appeal of the term "right" is obviously important? Here the careful reader of the book is likely to come away perplexed if not downright troubled.

Dr Gentile informs the reader that both the terms "ethics" and "morals" were rejected for the project and the reasons for this rejection are interesting. First, the book rejects the term "ethics" because these are viewed as "externally imposed rules" (27) and their connection with "seemingly sophistic reasoning exercises" (27). Morals, on the other hand are rejected because, even though "standards of right and wrong conduct" while "relevant to what we are talking about" emphasise "rightness" and "wrongness" of a particular behaviour "more than how we feel about that behavior. That is, the emphasis is on judgment and discipline more than on affirmative pursuit of desired goals and objects" (27). While noting that "all these terms overlap...the distinctions drawn here have as much to do with tone as with substance, but that tone is important" (27).

The next section of the GVV justification is important as it provides my main ground for criticism. It is also done so quickly that one can miss the importance of the next few steps.

The "fundamental stance" of GVV is said to be "values-driven action" that amounts to "alignment" which is defined as "... moving with our highest aspirations and our deepest sense of who we wish to be, rather than a stance of coercion and stern judgment, or of moving against our inclinations" (28). Significantly, we are informed that "[a]lthough self-discipline is certainly required to voice and act on our values, the emphasis here is on finding the part of ourselves that already wants to do this, and then empowering, enabling training, and strengthening that self" (28).

With respect to the meaning of "value" we are informed:

> The word "value" refers to the inherent worth and quality of a thing or an idea, and we often talk about valuing a challenging job, a comfortable lifestyle or even a well-made piece of clothing. However, the "values" we are discussing here are, in fact, values that most people would agree have a moral or ethical aspect to them. In this sense, these values are actually much the same as what we mean by "virtues". It's just that we are approaching them from a self-motivated aspirational stance, rather than a judgmental or self-disciplinary proposition. The word "value" is both a noun and a verb; it has inherent in it not only the concept of goodness − like "virtue" but also the act of wanting, desiring, or personally "valuing" something. So the choice of the term "values" is about tone and positioning, as well as literal definition" (28, emphasis added).

Then, conflating values that are "more profound" such as "access to the natural world, creativity, or dependability, independence or community" with those that are "not inherently moral" (such as well-made clothes) (29) the book, quoting a psychologist, suddenly discusses as an example of shared convergence across millennia, "virtue and strength" (29) and "six core virtues" that include "wisdom, courage, humanity, justice, temperance and transcendence" (29) and then what is said to be a "simpler put" list of "five widely shared values" that are "honesty, respect, responsibility, fairness and compassion" (29). There is no commentary on the shift between virtues and values and it is therefore implied either that virtues are irrelevant or that the two concepts are essentially the same thing.

I have spent some time on this to indicate two things. First, that "values" are said to be different from "ethics" and "morals" as they are "non-judgmental" and "self-aspirational" rather than "judgmental" and "self-disciplinary" and that these are essentially based upon "feelings" and the list of such things as "honesty" and "self-respect" and "fairness" are seen as widely shared "values" but not in any way related to or distinguished from the hard work of confirming habits to virtues that the virtue tradition took as a common starting point.

In short, the GVV project has chosen the language and strategies of the will, but without any moral tradition of the virtues, what they are, how they are approached and what is necessary in order to understand and gauge one's moral development are left completely undeveloped. GVV could be said to be "virtues lite" except that it isn't really about virtues at all.

More importantly, the invocation of "values" as if they have any necessarily shared moral content seems strange and rather haphazard to say the least. GVV is, after all, a program to teach about "values". If "values" is a relativistic and subjective category (as most philosophers allege) then what use can it have educationally or in relation to the virtue of shared community or a shared corporate project ? GVV gives us little to go on here. If, due to prior formation (When? How? How robust and coherent?) students have

certain moral beliefs and express these, according to the assumptions of the book this is just the sort of shared moral universe that
is adequate. How can that be?

In response to a reservation some have expressed to her in the
past about the mere articulation of "values" being "that we might
empower the wrong values" (45) the author states that "those
"wrong" values are already empowered" (45) and that "the goal
here is to raise the volume and increase the sophistication of
those arguments that are less often heard, that are less practised
and that can transform the workplace conversation" (45). Her
response about "prior empowerment" is not an adequate response
because the question was about content not the exercise of power.
That recourse to Marxist power categories is interesting and a
bit worrying since it elides a very real question about "wrong
values."

Looking into "wrong values" would, of course, require the
very searching moral and ethical evaluations that the book strives
to avoid yet precisely this is required to make the project morally
worthwhile at all. Simply too much is assumed in the glib avoidance
of judgment.

Near its conclusion, the book again sets out its goals that have:

> … been all about taking control of our own lives and careers.
> At heart it is based on the observation and conviction that
> choice exists: that we can choose not only when and how
> to voice and enact our values but, importantly, how to
> frame the choices so that we experience more degrees of
> freedom for doing so (220-221).

It is important to note that nowhere does Mary Gentile acknowledge the critiques of "values" referred to in the first part of this
paper. Interestingly, recent Catholic writers who not only support
her approach but advocate it as helpful for Catholic education and

state unequivocally that it is line with the teaching of Pope John Paul II, also do not mention the lineage of critiques of "values". It is as if the two worlds, that of philosophers aware of the dangers of values (first part above) and those who are sanguine about its so-called "inherent moral content" (following Wojtyła presumably) exist in parallel and have nothing to do with one another.[30] This sort of parallelism in relation to something as fundamental as the very integrity of the moral language being used is likely to further the confusion we have seen and that many learned commentators have noted above.

To make the point crystal clear. We cannot make "values" understood as objective simply by asserting that they are: that ship has sailed and it has nothing on it. The current use of "values' is made clear by legal theorist and philosopher Hans Kelsen in the following passage and at the very least it needs to be evaluated and

---

[30] Renee Kohler-Ryan and Sandy Lynch, "Values education and Christological personhood: Philosophical and practical implications" in Jānis (John) Tālivaldis Ozoliņš ed., *Civil Society, Education and Human Formation: Philosophy's Role in a Renewed Understanding of Education* (London: Routledge, 2017) 163-177. While the authors state near the end of their article that: "Fundamental to that [reflection on and evaluation of the modern social values] we would suggest, is the recognition of what a value is and what it is not" (175). Two problems exist with the analysis. First, this moral and ethical evaluation of "values" the authors say is fundamental is precisely what is *elided* by the very book the authors recommend as appropriate in a Catholic educational context. Second, in common with GVV the authors fail to note any difficulty or controversy with *the language of values itself*. As with Wojtyła himself the assumption that "values" are or should be *necessarily* what is good, a completely unjustified assumption, occludes the problem with the overall framework and its selection of the very term that eviscerates objective good due to the context of its exercise – "values". As noted above with respect to the work of Bernard Lonergan, it is said to be religious belief that makes "values" objective – how then when the surrounding culture in its scepticism *no longer shares conviction about the relevance of religious categories at all?* This is, in fact, our current condition and one I return to at the conclusion of this paper.

criticised by those who insist on using "values" as if they are personal, shared and inherently good:

> Value judgments, in contradistinction to statements about
> reality, have a purely subjective character. They are based
> on our wishes and fears, that is to say, on the emotion-
> al element of our consciousness. They are valid only for
> the judging subject, for they are not verifiable by facts.
> In this respect they differ essentially from the objective
> statements by which reality is described and explained,
> statements which are based on the rational element of our
> consciousness.[31]

## The problem with values is that it is a language that has *no* inherent or particular tradition

The language of "values" personal or shared gets us nowhere in
relation to objective goods or what is right and wrong. Saying
that "the wrong values are already empowered", as Gentile does,
or that transcendent good is implied in "values" as Wojtyła does,
is not helpful since we don't know what is "right" and "wrong"
about "values" in the first place. Despite its apparent main goal
of helping people in work environments to make present what
they believe to be right, which means, presumably, the good or

---

[31] Hans Kelsen, *The Political Theory of Bolshevism* (Berkeley: Univ. of Calif.
Press, 1959) 8. The fact/value distinction, the legacy of Hume, can only be
overcome, as various philosophers have demonstrated, by a robust purposive
conception of being itself. Phenomenology has been said to weaken conviction in being. That discussion is for another place but it is curious that when
purposiveness and a strong ontic philosophy is needed it will be found in
something that may benefit from, but must largely correct, any deficiencies in
phenomenology – one of which is clearly now evident in its endorsement of
"values" rather than an entailed choice for good in its very lexical formulations. Words matter profoundly in this area and "values" as a moral language
does not carry sufficient freight to act as a key term in a moral equation. See
on the ontological weaknesses of phenomenology, Stanley Jaki, *Means to
Message: A Treatise on Truth* (Grand Rapids: Eerdmans, 1999) 120, 127-128.

the true not simply what one wants (because it is said to be good for society and some "wants" clearly are not good for society), the jettisoning of both morals and ethics means that claims towards virtues are *subjectivised* into "mine" and not necessarily "yours" and they are *relativised* hence the book's continual avoidance of any correlation to the category of "morality" since that would amount to "judgmentalism". This is a book, remember, about the culture of corporations and their orientation to the moral goods and roles of business. This move to use a highly problematic and rejected language of "values" against an express rejection of a shared moral horizon is a very significant thing – particularly in a project that holds itself out as having major impacts around the world.[32]

The book lacks any discussion about any moral purpose for business and sets itself out as a program for individuals to, as the title suggests, "Give Voice to their personal Values". The necessary "goods" or "justice" or moral worth of what is being discussed is expressly avoided. Do we have the luxury as a society of this sort of preemptive avoidance of moral questions for business (or any other shared social) endeavor? Many would say "no". And it is not enough to say "oh well, the project of GVV is a small one" when it occupies the space that a larger project about morality and ethics might well fulfill. Giving Voice to *Virtues* might well be a useful project but that is not what is in the book on offer here.

---

[32] Asserting that "values" are or can be consistent with a communitarian or personalist ontology is merely that – an assertion; given the subjectivism inherent in "values" (since it is not an entailed language the way "virtues" are) it is completely random whether any particular user of "values" would be individualistic or personalist, selfish or other oriented. Education about justice (as what is due) human dignity, love, faith and compassion (under the rubric of "Grace perfecting nature") is of a different order of moral and educational clarity and alone can frame properly traditions of virtue and objective goods. The attempt by Catholic thinkers to assert the objective good of values, as an attempt to engage a culture using "values" in the subjective mode, can now be seen as an error.

This is not a light criticism when it is recalled that in the traditional categorisation the cardinal virtues are justice, wisdom, moderation and courage that were then said to be perfected by the theological virtues of faith, hope and love. Do we really want to start off a theory jettisoning these notions and the related insights that morality has to be taught, that it involves disciplines and acquired habits and it is against the standards of morality that laws are ultimately framed? And, having done so, how can we disambiguate the relativistic and subjectivist uses of "values" from these virtues that are deeply entailed and essentially and fundamentally about truth as understood within the Western and Catholic traditions? Silence about "virtues" or, worse, confusing them, as GVV does, with "values" (note its "lists" and the index entry "virtues: see values") only increases confusion.[33]

**What exactly is the problem with choosing the language of values for the GVV project and by extension, other values-based projects?**

What do "values" communicate exactly? They are about personal feelings and preferences just as GVV admits. We know that in the "values" world the first rule of "values" is: "you have your values and I have mine" and the second rule is that "you should not push

---

[33] One needs, here, to understand the argument of C.S. Lewis' *The Abolition of Man* (New York: Macmillan, 1943) which looks at world traditions and finds a significant amount of shared moral beliefs which he categorises as the "Tao" or "way" and which are a strong argument against the common misconception that moral beliefs are "relative" when there is strong evidence to the contrary. If we believe moral beliefs to be relative then we cannot have a commitment to "justice" shared by all global communities and we would not be able to subscribe to either of the main concepts in *The Universal Declaration of Human Rights* (1948) signed by most countries in the world, which endorses, at Article 1, moral concepts – "the dignity of the person" and "the brotherhood of man." These are not "universal values" because there are, in fact, no such things. As we have seen "values language" rejects the idea of shared moral goods as essential and necessary.

your values on me!" GVV complies with this understanding of "values." In failing to mention the criticisms of "the language of values" GVV and those who support it unwarily play into the very support for "gut feelings" and undifferentiated "empowerment" that make the project both superficially appealing to modern relativistic subjectivists (and big business and government) and utterly different from the moral projects that are needed to educate properly.

We like to think, as GVV likes to think, that these "values" concepts mean something because we want them personally. Our "values" should be honoured because they matter to us personally. But we also want them to mean something in a shared way. GVV says little about this dimension but Corporations like to indulge such things as "corporate values statements".

Joining shared nouns with the term "values" gives us the illusion that something specific is being shared. So we have such things as "Australian values", "Christian values", "family values" or "societal values" or "corporate values" or "transcendent values" as if they are shared and have meaning? But do they? Are they really shared? Moral analysis of possible positions needs to be undertaken and part of that involves an ethical and moral critique of the language of values itself – none of this, however, is on the table or even seen as necessary.

Let us give an example of contemporary "values language" in action. Australian politicians (in common with most politicians everywhere) seem enamoured of the general phrase in the vague way Orwell and many others have rejected: thus, in the recent election who did not hear politicians speak of "Australian values"? When the term is used, the audience nods knowingly … but what are they nodding to? On any particular issue: immigration, abortion, same-sex marriage, there is not just one "Australian value" at all! In fact, there are as many "Australian values" as there are Australians! So why do we derive comfort from this meaningless formulation and why might a politician like to use it? Why might a corporation like to speak of its "corporate values" while avoiding any moral articulation about public moral responsibilities or the common good?

Apart from lack of knowledge of the history and framework of a richer moral language such as virtues, perhaps they like the fact that such language obscures moral meaning and therefore not only proclamation of an inconvenient position and commitment but, perhaps, accountability in relationship to it. Let's look a little closer at how this works. Just recently, an example of the reason "values" cannot help us order the public sphere (much less the private) related to certain Muslims in Australia who did not want to sing the National Anthem.

A politician took up the case and in strong terms affirmed the importance of "Australian values" and the "Muslims" argued just as strenuously for "Muslim values" to be respected. A clash of values and a solution of power was all that could result. No one mentioned the idea of "civic virtues" and the importance of a moral nature to citizenship and what part and how far the idea of an anthem was necessary (if at all) to "civic friendship" and belonging. Values was simply, as Orwell says, "wind" – a loud noise ushering in force.

Empowerment, feelings, non-judgment, as in GVV all fit perfectly into the description of "emotivism" given by Alasdair MacIntyre in his landmark book *After Virtue*. MacIntyre reminds us that "emotivism" is "the doctrine that all evaluative judgments and more specifically all moral judgments are nothing but expressions of preference, expressions of attitude or feeling, in so far as they are moral or evaluative in character." [34] Is this not

---

[34] Alasdair MacIntyre, *After Virtue* (Notre Dame: Notre Dame University Press, 1984) 11-12 (emphasis in original).

exactly what we have seen in the project of GVV discussed above with its emphasis on following one's own feelings and not being "judgmental"?

Elsewhere in *After Virtue,* Alasdair MacIntyre addresses the attempt at various times in history to suggest "…the virtues are nothing but those qualities which we happen to find generally pleasant or useful." Commenting upon this "odd" suggestion, MacIntyre notes that:

> … what we find generally pleasant or useful will depend on what virtues are generally possessed and cultivated in our community. Hence the virtues cannot be defined or identified in terms of the pleasant or useful.[35]

Contemporary business studies, like contemporary studies in just about everything, have generally lost any connection to their disciplines as "moral" and, in so doing, must find something that stands in for moral evaluation. That is what GVV does in elevating "values" to a series of manipulative techniques. Starting with a non-judgmental completely self-generated set of "values" cut off from any necessarily objective sense of obligation (for that would be "judgmental") the "values" may or may not be related to anything at all since their grounding is based on personal choices rather than choices in relation to any objective goods or virtues. GVV finds that many people are pragmatists and then wants to appeal to their pragmatic side – but what, we may ask, do we do with those who simply want to maximise their own stake in a corporate world that has gone off the moral rails – such as Enron did some years ago? The GVV project, in avoiding the necessity of a moral understanding for business, plays into subjectivism, it doesn't challenge it at the root. Use of "values" by many in the Christian churches is forestalling an important alteration in moral education by perpetuating a serious confusion.

---

[35] Ibid., 160.

In common with many books written over the last thirty
or so years, GVV swims between "virtues" and "values" and,
erroneously, describes them as pretty much the same thing. Thus, it
is no surprise, but a considerable disappointment, to see that, in its
index, GVV defines "virtues" in this succinct and poignant manner:
"virtues: see values."!

Thus are the virtues and all that goes into, is entailed in, the
tradition of virtues, submerged under a sea of subjectivised feelings
where mere preferences of the will are expressly cut off from
"ethics", "morals" or even "virtues" themselves. What GVV does
is attempt to replace content with process and give the appearance
of guidance towards improvement (one could not call it in any
way moral improvement) with nothing in the way of substantive
guidance by using the unentailed language of "values".[36]

It is not so with the ancient framework of our Western tradition.
Here, "justice", the end of law, was a cardinal virtue – cardinal
from the word for "hinge" and a virtue because it is an end against
which our conduct can be evaluated. Justice, wisdom, courage
and moderation were deemed to be central virtues that could be
appreciated by reason and taught. It was an understanding of the

---

[36] The use of the concept of "entailed" and "unentailed" is more descriptive
than saying simply that "virtues" is a "thick" or "thin" language. Entailment
suggests what is true, that "virtues" are encapsulated over time in moral traditions and in relation to a constellation of meanings associated with that
tradition (cardinal virtues, theological virtues, related notions in the Christian
tradition of "Grace perfecting nature" and so on) whereas "values" have no
such entailment and since usually understood as personal preferences, need
have no settled or shared meanings at all. See, on "thick"and "thin" concepts in contrast to "values" as mere projections, Bernard Williams, *Ethics
and the Limits of Philosophy* (Cambridge: Harvard University Press, 1985)
129 ff. I would like to acknowledge useful discussions on these points with
Colleagues Dr Robert Anderson and Dr Steven Lovell-Jones, both of Notre
Dame, Sydney, and honours student Glynnis Nancarrow, all of whose concerns about "values language" mirror my own.

*telos* or moral purposes of conduct and habits that provides the way to evaluate the *techné* or techniques. Once this is understood, one can see how unhelpful the supposed substitution of "values" for "virtues" is. Values obliterate moral language. Recourse to "values", despite the best hopes of those who wish to use it otherwise, elevates the personal subjective based on "feelings" and leaves on the cutting floor any suggestion that there are "moral purposes" that we ought to pursue in common. What we are supposed to do when , for example, business simply runs rough-shod over reasonable moral positions? If we are, as the author of GVV states, not to be judgemental, ethical or moral or aspirational then how can we challenge wrong actions – after all we are supposed (but how) to know what is "right"?

The entire project of GVV starts off in mid-air and never lands on the moral ground necessary for moral education. What are we to do, for example, when a corporation is taken over by ideology? When a bank requires employees, for example, to endorse a position that a particular employee rejects for conscience reasons? The legal principle of accommodation here is not a "value" it is a moral obligation and that principle and its justice (understood as rendering what is due) require an understanding of the moral rules not a process of "values clarification" to sort out what is obligatory (and, yes, that is judgmental) for the corporation.

In fact, the project of GVV unwittingly supports the bracketing out of religion from the social sphere recommended by John Dewey in his framework. Dewey wishes to see religions drop any exclusive metaphysical claims that he says could not properly support "social values" since framed with religious presuppositions not shared by the non-religious. In exact opposition to the approach taken by Lonergan, above, Dewey wishes to strip religion of any of its claims to transcendence and uses the language of "heritage of values" and "social values" to do so:

... as long as social values are related to a supernatural
for which the churches stand in some peculiar way, there
is an inherent inconsistency between the demand and
efforts to execute it. On the other hand, it is urged that
the churches are going outside their special province when
they involve themselves in economic and political issues.
On the other hand, the very fact that they claim if not a
monopoly on supreme values and motivating forces, yet
a unique relation to them, makes it impossible for the
churches to participate in promotion of social ends on a
natural and equal human basis. The surrender of claims to
an exclusive and authoritative position is a *sine qua non* for
doing away with the dilemma in which churches now find
themselves in respect to their sphere of social action. ...I
cannot understand how any realisation of the democratic
ideal as a vital moral and spiritual ideal in human affairs is
possible without surrender of the conception of the basic
division to which supernatural Christianity is committed.[37]

It is ironic that the strategy in this Yale University Book from
1934, of bracketing out the "truth claims" of religion in order for
them to fit within the proper "heritage of values" of democracy, returns full circle in the Yale University Press book of three-quarters
of a century later, with its bracketing out of the "judgmental" and
the "aspirational". First religion is bracketed out by John Dewey
then coherent moral approaches are bracketed out by Mary Gentile
– the common denominator in both? The language of values.

---

[37] John Dewey, *A Common Faith* (New Haven: Yale UP, 1934) 83-84. Martha
Nussbaum, "Valuing Values: A Case for Reasoned Commitment", 6 *Yale J.L.
& Human* 197 (1994) in an article about "values" and normative judgment,
mentions Dewey but fails to note his method in relation to values. Dewey as
a proto-Rawlsian, bracketing religion out of public life, is simply offering an
American application of the strategy of George Jacob Holyoake, see Iain T.
Benson "Considering Secularism" in Douglas Farrow ed. *Recognizing Reli-
gion in a Secular Society* (Montreal: McGill-Queens, 2004) 83-98.

## Conclusion: Can anything be salvaged from values language?

The GVV project fails to address the deepest needs of the collapse of ethics in our time and the replacement of genuine moral languages with the subjectivised language of the will that is "values" language. While "values" may be said to be perfectly valid when discussing matters that are about personal preference, choices relating to clothes, or food or musical preference may in fact be perfectly framed by "values" but that is its limit.

If we want, in business, in law, in medicine, in economics, in politics, in philosophy and in theology itself, to have a moral language that engages what is right in all these disciplines understood as the human choices of the acting person towards shared moral purposes, we cannot rely on merely the personal language of preference to do so. It is a pseudo-moral language – it could even be argued that it is an anti-moral language since what is moral is not merely personal and any meaningful idea of "right" that is not just "might" is due to its being evaluated beyond the category of choice itself. But this is what the book and the project specifically avoid and why the use of this sort of framework is inconsistent with a deeply Catholic approach to the teaching of morals or ethics.

GVV's strategy of bracketing out "ethics" and "morals" as "judgmental" sets us on the path to supposedly non-judgmental evaluation but this is not only impossible, it is, as some others have noted, unwise.[38] It is impossible because to evaluate is, by

---

[38] Tracy L. Gonzalez-Padron, O.C. Ferrell, Linda Ferrell, Ian A. Smith, "A Critique of Giving Voice to Values Approach to Business Ethics Education, *Journal of Academic Ethics*, December 2012, Vol. 10, Issue 4, 251-269 are critical of the assumption of adequate moral training inherent in the GVV approach. The authors also criticise GVV as being "not a comprehensive or holistic approach" The critique I am mounting here is much deeper as it looks at the very language of axiology itself. For an axiological analysis that fails to examine the problems of "values language" raised here, but that is helpful in many other respects, see: Ramon M. Lemos, *The Nature of Value* (Gainsville:

definition, to judge and the obscuring of this necessity of judgment may fit the current trend towards so-called "neutral" evaluation, but it is both philosophically bankrupt and culturally naïve. It might even be suicidal.[39]

There is little merit in creating processes that amount to the assertion of the will by other languages and using other techniques. To the person who is being manipulated by those who know how to use a process to do so, (the "already empowered") and where moral

University Press of Florida, 1995). See also, for an attempt to relate axiology to more traditional "ethics" Vernon J. Bourke, *Ethics in Crisis* (Milwaukee: Bruce, 1966) 36-38. More detailed work than I have briefly sketched with reference to Wojtyła is needed to trace the origins of "values language" into the Roman Catholic Church, most likely through the phenomenologists and its use by many leading Catholic thinkers including Jacques Maritain, Bernard Lonergan, Dietrich von Hildebrand, Hans Urs von Balthasar and John Paul II. The attempt to use this language, assuming that "values" are necessary related to objective goods and in the (mistaken) belief that it would engage surrounding cultures who were using "values" as we have seen in morally obscuring ways, has resulted, not in engagement, but in increasing confusion as to the tradition of the Church itself. An excellent example of this confusion is, as set out above, to be found in the attempt in the *Compendium of the Social Doctrine of the Church* (Washington, D.C.: United States Conference of Catholic Bishops, 2009) to set out the relationship between "principles and values" at #197. The effort conflates some virtues, with things that are not virtues and what were known as the theological virtues with the cardinal ones and with certain aspects (freedom) that are not virtues at all. Instead of clarity, Dewey's category of "social values" is re-employed in a religious context but this time further confusing the moral language used formerly. Attempts, such as that by Thomas D. Williams, see footnote 5, with respect, to support John Paul II's use of "values", are unconvincing and misconceived.

[39] This language is justified when one thinks that such things as the environment and the development of weapons are, in fact, restricted or managed by moral claims in relation to what nations and citizens should do and refrain from doing. Much of the language of international diplomacy requires recognition of and adherence to moral notions (consider, for a recent example amongst many, "the responsibility to protect" which came into the world communities in the year 2000): see, Stephen Hall, *Principles of International Law* (Australia: Lexis Nexis, 20164, 54th ed.) 458-461, 482-483.

arguments have been, supposedly, put to one side, certain outcomes are likely to occur.

First, the task of evaluation against a genuinely moral ground is removed (we are not to be "judgmental"remember?) and, second, manipulation replaces open moral discussion and arguments. This is not an advance at all from moral drift, it is just giving us the illusion that we have a map. But this is a map of a particular sort – one in which you yourself decide where the points of the compass are not any reality "out there." Such a form of navigation is hardly useful and likely dangerous.

"Values" is the language of "preference" – the language of "I want" not the language of "I should". It is confused, relativistic and a mask for the pernicious doctrine of "might is right." "Values" are not, despite what the book and its project or supporters might mislead us into thinking "the same as virtues"; "values" and "virtues" are utterly different creatures. Virtues are thick and entailed and have a content and long traditions spanning countries, philosophies and religions; values are thin, unentailed, and, well, whatever one wishes them to be. The choice of using "values" language within the Catholic tradition in the 20th century, often by leading Catholic thinkers, turns out from the perspective of the 21st century to be misconceived. Instead of connecting the tradition of virtues and objective goods with the times, it subjectivised and relativised the tradition by using the corrupted lexicon of the times.

What is involved in rejecting "values language" is not, as some allege, "banishing a word" in an unscholarly manner, but, rather, employing scholarship in order to see through a language that in its nature contains a deliberate or unintentional ambiguity that obscures shared moral meanings.[40] It is helpful to recall that John

---

[40] In their book on the thinning of education – one aspect of which is the employment of "values language" in what purport to be courses on ethics or morals, see: Peter C. Emberley and Waller R. Newell, *Bankrupt Education: The Decline of Liberal Education in Canada* (Toronto: University of Toronto

Stuart Mill, one of the fathers of liberalism, and whose project, according to Maurice Cowling,[41] was in essence a replacement strategy for religion, and who was certainly no friend of objective virtues (and who wrote before the neologism "values" was created) had wise things to say about terminology when it ceased to be clear. As Hugo Meynell points out, in his *System of Logic* Mill describes the need to redefine a term that has ceased to have any determinative meaning due to its becoming applied to a heterogenous collection of things with nothing in common. If this is not done, according to

Press, 1994) where, at 132 the authors note: "..the genie is out of the bottle: modern man has discovered the dread truth that values are indeed relative. He will never be able to escape this knowledge. Not only do we have to create something completely unpredictable, but we have to do so in the knowledge that it is a value, rather than an absolute truth." As GVV and its employment in a Catholic setting shows, however, some modern people, in this case educators, appear to have somehow escaped the knowledge that "values are indeed relative." What appears to be happening is that the use by some of "values" in aid of what they hope or believe to be objective uses of the term is not being heard or picked up as such a use by those outside the specialised use of "values" in this way. As the majority of philosophers of contemporary culture are aware, values *connote* and increasingly *denote* not just a personal subjective use and evaluation but a *relativistic* one. It is the failure to note that both connotative and denotative aspects alike are, or have become to most people, subjective and relativistic, that makes the use of "values" by those who still believe the term to be "moral" such an unusual part of this current confusion. Simply stating that "values" are objective is just wishful thinking and if it could ever have been said with confidence it cannot, as so many have argued, be said any longer.

[41] Maurice Cowling, *John Stuart Mill on Liberalism* (Cambridge: Cambridge University Press, 1971) xii. On the tendency of "liberalism" to foster, from its inception, an extremely illiberal form, see John Gray, *Two Faces of Liberalism* (New Press: London, 2001). See, also, in a legal context Barry W. Bussey "The Charter is not a Blueprint for Moral Conformity" in Iain T. Benson and Barry W. Bussey (eds.), *Religion, Liberty and the Jurisdictional Limits of Law* (Toronto: LexisNexis, 2017) 367-414. Professor Bussey explains the use and criticisms, some from within the judiciary itself, to the recent creation and use of "Charter values" at 393 ff.

Mill, the heterogenous term is no longer of any use in thought and communication.[42] So, long before its current placement in books that are supposedly guides to help us effectuate "right" under the guise of "values" J.S. Mill had, himself, provided a strong argument for values being well past its "best by" date.

The task of understanding and passing on shared moral meanings is, in fact, the whole purpose of anything purporting to be genuinely moral and ethical: what a "values based" project is actually doing is anyone's guess. For those who have used this bankrupt language in their work, thinking it was engaging or "useful", the road ahead is clear. First to admit frankly that mistakes were and are being made in using "values language", thinking it can serve moral ends; second to find ways to articulate for our time moral lessons and languages that keep *techné* related to *telos* and that frame the virtues in their proper relationships with one another as describing shared moral goals and the acts of persons as moral choices, not merely values.

Writing long before his more famous later works, Alasdair MacIntyre once described, in startlingly presient ways, and without using the language of "values" where that language would lead. Writing of our moral vocabulary, he notes:

> To understand that generosity or courage or thrift is a virtue is to understand that one ought to be generous or brave or thrifty, and this 'ought' has a force prior to any choice of moral standards that we make. Indeed choices of moral standards are judged correct or incorrect in the light of their understanding of the virtues and vices. There are, however, other individuals who have a different kind of moral vocabulary. They do not belong to a single homogenous moral community with a shared language and shared

---

[42] Hugo Meynell, *Freud, Marx and Morals* (London: MacMillan Press Ltd., 1981) 172, citing J.S. Mill, *System of Logic,* I, viii.7 at 204.

concepts. Instead they find themselves solicited from different standpoints ...The fact that there are these two sorts
of people in our society underlies the paradoxical element
in many moral discussions ... on the one side there is the
claim that our key moral expressions are and cannot ever
be anything more than the expression of the agent's own
choice of standards, that they have no more authority over
the agent than the agent himself chooses to confer upon
them; and on the other view is that if we take, for example,
the virtue words, words such as "courage", "generosity",
and "cowardice", we shall find that the rules for the use of
these expressions are such that we cannot choose what is
to count as courageous, or what is to count as cowardly,
but we have to accept a framework of concepts which is
given in our moral vocabulary. This argument is very often
presented as though each side was claiming to characterise
the whole range of moral concepts, as these must be in all
times and all places, in such a way that one side must be altogether right and the other must be altogether wrong; but
if one looks sociologically at the facts about this particular
society now, the suspicion is born that what we find in this
dispute are perhaps not two rival descriptions of the same
moral phenomena, but instead, descriptions of two quite
different sets of phenomena, which do as a matter of fact
coexist without our society.[43]

---

[43] Alasdair MacIntyre, *Secularization and Moral Change* (London: Oxford
University Press, 1967) 51-53. This is not the place to go through all of MacIntyre's elegant and nuanced argument but the entire book is relevant to the
theme of this paper and his point that there are in fact "two kinds of moral vocabulary" one based essentially on conformance to "the good" and the other
based on subjective choosing: "this is what I choose to approve of" brilliantly
tracks "virtues" in contradistinction to "values"; it is extraordinary that he
does not speak of "values" at all in the book yet a contemporary reader will
note that is exactly what he is describing. MacIntyre anticipated the confusion around "values" with an uncanny prophetic realisation that sophisticated
attempts to replace "this is good" with "this is the exercise of my values"

The entire book is relevant to the central theme of this paper but its conclusion suggests something of the first importance. MacIntyre suggests nothing less than that the loss of moral vocabulary is itself both reflective of *but causative of the general loss of faith in religion*. In other words, though he does not mention the word "values" as can be seen from the quotation above, so perfect does the term fit his criticism of subjectivism that it is important to see how the argument fits what I have been describing in this paper. He states:

> If it is true that without established moral agreement the notion of moral authority is vacuous, then light is thrown both upon the history of the Church's loss of moral authority and also upon certain contemporary religious claims. For it is not the case that men first stopped believing in God and in the authority of Church, and then subsequently started behaving differently. It seems clear that men first of all lost any over-all social agreement as to the right ways to live together, and so ceased to be able to make sense of any claims to moral authority. Consequently they could not find intelligible the claims to such authority which were advanced on the part of the Church. The historical evidence about the development of secularisation bears this out. Social change and with it moral change is chronologically prior to the loss of belief effected by intellectual argument...*English society today is at best morally pluralistic in a way that makes the notion of authoritative moral utterance inapplicable; at worst it is a society in which the lack of a shared moral vocabulary makes the use of explicit moral assertion positively pernicious.* What is pernicious is the illusion that is created of a society united not as

---

is not a development of but a radical departure from and destruction of the moral tradition of virtues. It is a tragedy that Catholic thinkers from popes and bishops to contemporary educators have not learned this lesson.

in fact it is by harsh utilitarian necessities, but by common standards and ideas.[44]

If MacIntyre is correct, and the weight of other writers covered in this article support his claims, then the problem of values language with its corroding effects on a shared moral and ethical lexicon is likely central to the loss of religious faith generally in modernity. While no single cause is likely to have led to the great diremptions of modernity, *the incoherence of moral discourse* at the heart of the tradition that had nurtured coherent virtues language for so long, Roman Catholicism must lie close to the centre of our current confusions. And this confusion persists to this day in the persistence of "values language" in Catholic education and the pronouncements of clerics and academics in Catholic institutions. Parallelism, as I have described it, is a cause and continuing interference to reformulating moral language; confusion the result, and engagement and clarification the only possible solutions to our moral lexical dilemmas.

Books of approaches that further parallelism and confusion may be useful but only in *de-constructing the purported utility* of values language. This is what I have attempted to do in this paper. A more detailed work is needed to explain how the cuckoo's egg got laid into the Catholic lexical nest in the first place; but that is not this article.

This article is essentially about a problem at the heart of the Catholic Church as much as of Western Cultures. The criticisms it levels, since the language it abominates is ubiquitous and used, as Grant noted above, by many who either don't know that it undercuts their beliefs or deny it does so, may cause some to react defensively, I would like to conclude by quoting the wise words of a Catholic philosopher of an earlier time – Etienne Gilson, who wrote once in a different but related context:

---

[44] Ibid. 54-57 (emphasis added).

I have said elsewhere that an honest and open disagreement is of more use to philosophy than an illusory reconciliation which masks basic differences ... Philosophy deals with necessities of thought that cannot be compromised. No matter how painful it may be, a dispute is respectable if it is honest. It is impossible to tolerate, in all honesty, the least confusion if one truly believes that the principles of knowledge itself are at stake. In such a case the effort to attain a pure metaphysical position requires a search for formulas free from all taint of compromise.[45]

The principles of knowledge about morality and the ability to maintain a tradition of virtues is what is at stake where the obscuring language of "values" is present. As noted earlier, we are on the wrong road if we use "values" as it does the opposite of connect with the surrounding cultures. As both George Grant and Alasdair MacIntyre have said, it obscures morality and is related to a loss of purpose, clarity and religious faith itself. The issue is fundamental and long past critical. The sooner we get the cuckoo's eggs out of the nest the better.

Iain.benson@notredame.edu.au

---

[45] Etienne Gilson (transl. Mark A. Wauck) *Thomist Realism and the Critique of Knowledge* (San Francisco: Ignatius Press, 1986) 25.

# 2

# EDUCATION AND THE CULTURE OF FREEDOM

## Kevin Donnelly

What is the purpose of education and what does it meant to be educated? How such questions are answered is more than academic as whatever happens in schools, especially the formal school curriculum, implicitly or explicitly embodies a particular educational philosophy.

Given the compulsory nature of school education and the fact, in addition to the family, that schools are one of the most influential institutions that determine how individuals perceive themselves and their place in the wider society and the world at large it is especially vital that such questions are addressed.

Based on an analysis of various state, territory and national intended curriculum syllabuses, frameworks and related documents undertaken as part of the 2014 review of Australian National Curriculum it is possible to identify 5 approaches that have influenced curriculum development since the late 60s.

One model adopts a child-centred view of education where what is taught is based on the world of the student and what is often immediately local, contemporary and relevant. A second approach, based on a Marxist critique of capitalist society and a rainbow alliance of cultural-left theories, argues that education must be used to overthrow the status quo and bring about radical change.

Preparing students for the workforce and future careers represents a third approach; one where the focus is on increased productivity and wealth and ensuring that students become productive members of the workforce. Related to this utilitarian view of education is the argument that the curriculum must embrace 21st century competencies and skills given the impact of the new technologies and the advent of the digital age.

Enculturation, where the culture of a particular community and society is internalised by each succeeding generation, represents a fifth approach to addressing the question of the purpose of education and what it means to be educated.

Within the context of Western civilisation and those countries associated with the Anglo-sphere, including England, Australia, America, New Zealand and Canada, enculturation also refers to a liberal view of education associated with Matthew Arnold's phrase in *Culture and Anarchy* "the best which has been thought and said in the world".

While the five various approaches to the curriculum are important it is possible to argue that enculturation involving a liberal education is preeminent as it is best placed to contribute to the emotional, spiritual, moral and intellectual development of individuals and the health and wellbeing of society and the culture at large.

Adopting a child-centred view of education and ensuring that the curriculum, especially during the early years of primary school, relates to and draws on the world of the individual learner can be beneficial. If learning is overly abstract and distant then students often find it difficult to understand or to see what is being taught as engaging and relevant.

At the same time given that each individual's knowledge, understanding and experience, by necessity, is limited and enculturation does not happen intuitively or by accident, it is vital that the curriculum broadens and enriches by introducing students to what is unknown and foreign.

As argued by the American academic E.D. Hirsch and based on the concept of cultural literacy restricting learning to what is contemporary often leads to a superficial and limited educational experience.

In history, for example, always focusing on studying the local community or contemporary events denies the ability to appreciate and understand the significance and impact of important historical events that have shaped Western civilisation and Australia's development as a nation.

If the only literary works students encounter are contemporary and restricted to their immediate environment then they will remain ignorant of the great literary texts from the past that have stood the test of time and that have something profound and meaningful to say about human nature and our relationship to what D.H. Lawrence terms the "circumambient universe, at the living moment".

It also must be noted, with only minor exceptions, that mastering complex mathematical algorithms, learning a foreign language or how to analyse and appreciate literary works such as Shakespeare's tragedies requires being taught by those expert in the area and acknowledging the contributions of those who have gone before.

The aphorism often attributed to Isaac Newton that "If I have seen further it is by standing on the shoulders of giants" recognises that particular disciplines are not rediscovered afresh with each succeeding generation but are part of an evolving dialogue that is ongoing and that stretches into the distant past.

While child-centred learning can be traced by to the rise of the progressive education movement during the late 60s and early 70s, a time of de-schooling, community schools and open classrooms, a more recent variation relates to what is described as 'personalised learning'.

In addition to placing the interests and world of the child centre stage personalised learning embraces the internet and computers on the basis that today's children are "digital natives" and the new technologies offer a dynamic, flexible and innovative way to learn. Instead of teachers teaching in a more formal sense they become 'facilitators' and 'guides by the side' as self-directed learning takes precedence.

Drawing largely on the new sociology of education movement and cultural-left academics and activists such as Antonio Gramsci, Louis Althusser, Pierre Bourdieu, Foucault and M.F.D. Young the second approach to education represents a Marxist critique of the nature of knowledge and the relationship between schools and society.

Whereas a liberal view of education considers the various disciplines as inherently worthwhile and central in the search for wisdom and truth, academics like M.F.D. Young argue that they are "socio-cultural" constructs that reinforce the hegemony of the ruling elites. What constitutes knowledge is part of the "ideological state apparatus" employed by those more powerful in society to ensure they maintain their domination and control over the less privileged.

A belief in meritocracy, academic studies and that learning can be objective, impartial and valued for its own sake are condemned and deconstructed in terms of power relationships based on the new trinity of "gender, ethnicity and class".

The one-time Victorian Premier and education minister, Joan Kirner, best sums up this radical approach to education in a speech delivered to the Victorian Fabian society in which argues schools and the curriculum must be "[p]art of the socialist struggle for equality, participation and social change, rather than an instrument of the capitalist system".

More recent additions to a Marxist critique of schooling and society is a rainbow alliance of cultural-left theories including: Neo-

Marxism, postmodernism, deconstructionism, feminism and gender, queer and post-colonial theories. While often in disagreement what all hold in common is a hostility towards a liberal view of education and the belief that knowledge is inherently worthwhile and that there are objective, impartial truths.

As noted by Frank Furedi in *Where Have All The Intellectuals Gone?* the end result is that "Truth is rarely represented as an objective fact; it is frequently portrayed as the product of subjective insight, which is in competition with other equally valid perspectives". Associated with the belief that there are no self-evident truths is cultural relativism based on the assumption that all cultures are of equal value and worth.

The critique of a liberal view of education associated with Western civilisation that draws on Marxism and theory is best illustrated by long march through tertiary institutions as a result of the 1960's cultural revolution. On American campuses, as detailed in Roger Kimball's *The Long March*, Allan Bloom's *The Closing of the American Mind* and Dinish D'Souza's *Illiberal Education*, cultural-left radicals mounted a scathing critique of a liberal education.

The way history was taught was attacked as Eurocentric, racist, sexist and guilty of either marginalising or ignoring minority and disadvantaged groups. The type of literature associated with the Western canon was also condemned for being Eurocentric and for being male dominated and for reinforcing the status quo and failing to teach what become known as "critical literacy".

More recent examples of the cultural-left's success in its long march through schools and universities include "trigger warnings" and "microaggression". Trigger warnings involve warning minority and oppressed individuals that what they are about to encounter might cause offence or distress.

Microaggression, as opposed to displaying overt prejudice or bias, is when somebody's actions or inactions offends in an indirect and less obvious way less advantaged individuals or groups such as women, those of non-white ethnicity or race and LGBTQI people.

Australian universities have also suffered as a result of the long march and the impact of cultural-left theories. The Australian academic Pierre Ryckmans in the ABC's 1996 Boyer Lectures argues that the dominance of theory has led to a situation where it is impossible to make judgements of relative value or to be objective. As a result, Ryckmans concludes "to deny the existence of objective values is to deprive the university of its spiritual means of operation".

John Carroll, an Emeritus Professor at La Trobe University, when discussing what he describes as "cultural masochism" in an essay published in a September 2015 edition of *Quadrant*, also expresses concerns about the impact of theory on tertiary education.

When detailing what he sees as the existential malaise suffered by Western culture Carroll argues "Much of the intelligentsia has turned against the long Western high-cultural tradition that since Homer and Plato has sought the true, the beautiful and the good. It has rather set to criticising its society – customs, traditions and institutions".

An example of this critique of a liberal view of education is Omid Tofighian's condemnation of what is described as "whiteness" in the curriculum. Tofighian, from the University of Sydney and in a comment piece on The Conversation website, criticises "whiteness" as being "Eurocentric" and guilty of "racism, sexism, classism, historical injustice and prejudice based on religion".

"Whiteness", according to Tofighian, is "non-inclusive" as it normalises "exclusionary practices" and the solution is to "dismantle the white curriculum" and validate the "identity and cultural background of marginalised groups".

A third approach to defining the purpose of education and what it means to be educated involves a utilitarian approach associated with ensuring the students are prepared for the world of work. While the school curriculum, and education more broadly, has always involved preparing students for a trade, career or profession there was a recognition that enculturation involving a liberal view of education was equally, if not more, important.

Not so with the belief that the primary task of education is to produce a workforce that is effective in contributing to the nation's productivity, economic growth and prosperity. Best illustrated by the 1992 Key Competencies report (otherwise known as the *Mayer Report*) the belief is that the subjects associated with the established school curriculum are less important than dealing with employment related competencies.

The chair of the report, Eric Mayer, argues that what are described as key competencies "are fundamental to our future economic competitiveness" and that "Australia's ability to compete internationally will be enhanced if the Key Competencies are acquired by our young people".

The seven competencies identified in the Mayer Report include: collecting, analysing and organising information, communicating ideas and information, planning and organising activities, working with others in teams, solving problems, using mathematical ideas and techniques and using technology.

The Australian national curriculum, currently being implemented in all state and territory schools, offers a variation of the Mayer competencies when it argues in favour of what are described as "general capabilities". The Australian Curriculum and Reporting Authority describes these capabilities as involving "an integrated and interconnected set of knowledge, skills, behaviours and dispositions that can be developed and applied across the curriculum".

When justifying its emphasis on embedding general capabilities across the school curriculum ACARA argues their purpose is to "add richness and depth to the learning areas and help students see the interconnectedness of their learning".

A fourth approach to the purpose of education and also utilitarian in nature is so-called 21st century learning where the need, according to a 2015 paper published by the Queensland Curriculum & Assessment Authority, is to enable students to "succeed in a complex, competitive, knowledge-based, information-age, technology driven economy and society".

The Queensland education authority argues 21st century skills are much needed as they reflect the changing world and "differ from those skills needed in the past". As a result, students are required to be "lifelong learners", "global citizens" and "technology savvy, problem solvers". Ignored is that information is not knowledge and understanding is not wisdom and no amount of searching the web can take the place of being educated in its fullest and most enriching sense.

Megan O'Connell from the Mitchell Institute at Victoria University puts a similar case for the importance of 21st century learning when she argues "Our education system was formed in the manufacturing era" and that "Young people need different skill sets to what is taught in the traditional curriculum if they are to thrive in high-tech, global, competitive job markets".

As to what constitutes 21st century capabilities a report by the Mitchell Institute authored by Torii and O'Connell lists them as: critical thinking, problem solving, creativity, curiosity, interpersonal and communications skills, teamwork and craftsmanship".

When detailing the purpose of education a fifth approach involves enculturation; a process whereby each succeeding generation is initiated into the culture in which they are born and which they are expected to live. Within the context of Western civilisation, as previously mentioned, enculturation generally involves a liberal education.

Brian Crittenden describes a liberal education as a "broad introduction to those major aspects of literate culture in which human beings have most significantly expressed their intellectual, imaginative and emotional capacities".

Central to this liberal view of education is the belief, in the words of T.S. Eliot, that it "should stand for preservation of learning, for the pursuit of truth, and in so far as men are capable of it, the attainment of wisdom".

While often criticised for being obsolete and unchanging it is important to note that Matthew Arnold also describes a liberal education as "turning a fresh and free thought upon our stock notions and habits, which we now follow staunchly but mechanically".

The focus is on change as well as continuity as the various disciplines and areas of learning change and evolve over time. A liberal education is also based on the belief that how we perceive the world is not simply subjective as there are objective truths that better explain the nature of reality and the word in which we exist.

The commitment to objectivity and empiricism also suggests that not all knowledge is a socio-cultural construct and that it is wrong to argue education and schooling are instruments used by those more powerful in society to dominate and control disadvantaged and minority individuals and groups.

If all knowledge is relative or a reflection of power relationships then it would be impossible to properly weigh and evaluate different points of view or disagreements concerning what is true or what is false. This is apart from the fact that a good deal of what constitutes a liberal education is directed at questioning and critiquing the status quo.

Education in its truest sense is not indoctrination as central to its task is promoting the individual's ability to weigh conflicting viewpoints, to critically examine contentious issues and to recognise when opinions and beliefs are either supported by the available evidence or are not.

A liberal education, in part due to the influence of Christianity, is also inherently moral where students are taught what constitutes good and bad behaviour, what characterises the good life and how best to contribute to the common good. Much of the Western literary canon, for example, details and explores the nature of good and evil and the consequences of one's thoughts, emotions and actions.

A liberal education, unlike generic competencies and skills, is also grounded in the established disciplines and areas of knowledge on the belief that the ability to think critically, to solve problems and to be creative are subject specific. Analysing a poem is very different to solving a mathematical algorithm or evaluating the importance of a significant historical event.

As argued by the American academic E.D. Hirsch, "The real-life competencies that people need, such as the abilities to read, to write, to communicate, to learn, to analyze, and to grasp and manipulate mathematical symbols, have major components that psychologists have found to be domain-specific".

Unlike contemporary approaches to education associated with child-centred, personalised learning it is also true that a liberal education requires humility, civility and a willingness to postpone immediate gratification for what can often be difficult, time consuming and onerous.

In Pierre Ryckman's ABC Boyer Lectures previously referred to he puts the argument that it is critically important for students to appreciate and be knowledgeable about their own culture before they learn about others. He states, "You cannot usefully approach a foreign culture – specifically a rich and sophisticated foreign culture – if you do not first have a firm grasp of your own culture".

In the context of Australia and other countries that have grown out of Western civilisation central to this process of enculturation is experiencing a liberal education; one that not only addresses education in its richest and most fulfilling sense but also one that introduces students to an on-going conversation stretching back to the early Roman and Greek sophists and philosophers.

## Bibliography

Arnold, M. 1969 (edition). *Culture & Anarchy*. Great Britain. Cambridge University Press.

Bloom, A. 1987. *The Closing of the American Mind*. New York, Simon and Schuster.

Carroll, J. 2015. "Why the West Wants to Lose." Quadrant Online. September 2015. Retrieved 16 August 2017 from https://quadrant.org.au/magazine/2015/09/west-wants-lose/

Crittenden, B. 1996. *Thinking about Education*. South Melbourne, Longman.

D' Souza, D. 1998. *Illiberal Education*. New York. The Free Press.

Furedi, F. 2004. *Where Have All The Intellectuals Gone?*. London. Continuum.

Hirsch, E.D. 1996. *The Schools We Need and Why We Don't Have Them*. New York. Anchor Books.

Kimball, R. 2000. *The Long March*, San Francisco, Encounter Books.

Kirner, J. 1983. "Choice, privilege and equality – the socialist dilemma?" in Victorian Fabian Society Pamphlet 41 *Education – Where From? Where To?* Melbourne. Victorian Fabian Society.

Lawrence, D.H. 1925. "Morality and the Novel". In Beal, A (Ed). 1967. *Selected Literary Criticism. D.H. Lawrence*. London. Heinemann Educational Books.

Mayer, E. 1992. *Competencies*. Australian Education Council and Ministers of Vocational Education, Employment and Training. Australia.

O'Connell, M. 2017. "Experts agree: schools not preparing students for twenty-first century". Mitchell Institute Media Release, dated 27 March 2017. Retrieved 1 August 2017 from http://www.mitchellinstitute.org.au/media-releases/experts-agree-schools-not-preparing-students-for-twenty-first-century/

Queensland Curriculum & Assessment Authority, 2015. *21st century skills for senior education*. QCAA, Brisbane.

Torii, K. and O'Connell, M. *Preparing Young People for the Future of Work*. Mitchell Institute Policy Paper No. 01/2017. Melbourne. Mitchell Institute.

Ryckmans, P. 1996. *The View from the Bridge: Aspects of Culture*. The 1996 Boyer Lectures. Sydney. Australian Broadcasting Commission.

Tofighian, O. 2015. "To tackle extremism in schools we must challenge the white curriculum". *The Conversation*. Retrieved 17 August, 2017 from https://theconversation.com/to-tackle-extremism-in-schools-we-must-challenge-the-white-curriculum-48316

Young, M.F.D. (Ed). 1971. *Knowledge and Control*. London. Collier Macmillan.

# 3

# LIBERAL EDUCATION AND THE GOOD LIFE:

## Christopher Dawson and the Role of Human Migration and Diffusion in the Life and Study of Culture

*James Gaston*

### Introduction

It is an honour to be here with all of you today. Before I begin my presentation I wish to thank my good friend, Dr David Daintree, and The Christopher Dawson Centre for Cultural Studies for inviting me to take part in the Centre's 2017 Colloquium. As Dr Daintree has clearly noted in our theme, a proper understanding of liberal education is essential if we are to foster the good life in general and especially if we are to do so within the context of modern society. This Colloquium marks an important step in our continuing deliberation on such matters, and it is a pleasure to join all of you in this vital endeavor. The title of my paper is Liberal Education and the Good Life: Christopher Dawson, and the Role of Human Migration and Diffusion in the Life and Study of Culture. I will address our theme by way of an especial emphasis on the nature of a culture and the dynamic aspects of cultural change.

Throughout the history of mankind the movement of peoples and the ensuing cultural interaction has played a profound role in the life and development of societies and cultures.[1] In fact, aside

---

[1] Christopher Dawson often uses interchangeably the terms "culture" and "society". All human groups constitute societies, but the cultural expression

from the primary role of religion, such human diffusion may well constitute the second most important formative influence in the social life of man. However, the scale and the impact of modern migration, and the manifold ramifications associated with it, go well beyond anything witnessed thus far in human history. If man is to live a good life in the present globalized world, he must assess the present, as all wise men do, in light of the past and the eternal. And in today's world that effort requires, among other things, a renewed understanding of the effect of modern education on the study of the nature of human culture and cultural change, with especial attention to the extensive impact of modern migration and diffusion.

The myriad current national and international policy debates regarding worldwide human migration play no role per se in this work, nor do the statistical analyses of demographic, political, economic, natural resource or other such empirical data. Rather, this is an attempt to consider the dynamics of cultural change as an important example of how modern education diminishes our reflection on the good life, because it fails to be truly liberal and holistic in its treatment of the common and foundational elements of human cultural life. This paper seeks to address this inadequacy as do the other excellent presentations in this colloquium.

The thesis of this argument is therefore the following. A truly liberal and holistic educational paradigm is essential if we are to reflect justly upon the qualities of the good life. Such an educational model will succeed only to the extent that it focuses upon human culture. And that a proper grasp of the nature and formation of

---

of such groups varies, as do the social science concepts and terminology that address them. Dawson, as a cultural historian and sociologist, generally considers a society to be a more refined, more rational and complex form of culture, as expressed, for example, in a civilization. A more extensive consideration of such distinctions is found Chapter I of Jacques Maritain, *Man and the State* (Chicago: University of Chicago Press, 1951).

human culture, including the role of migration and diffusion in cultural change, is indispensable to any valid interpretation of human society. In the process, some of the characteristic qualities of modern life will be assessed. Christopher Dawson's vision of liberal education, including the meaning and matter of culture, is central to this effort, and the argument will be framed primarily in light of his thought.

Dawson was one of the most brilliant and comprehensive thinkers in the Western tradition. Regardless, it is important to emphasise that he was first and foremost a cultural historian. He was truly a Catholic humanitarian and intellectual in that he strove to study the human condition in its most comprehensive and realistic expression so as to grasp as fully as possible the true nature, life and end of man. Like many of his contemporaries, Dawson was concerned with what was often referred to as the 20th Century crisis of Western Civilization. He feared we had arrived at a crucial turning point in the history of the West and the world, due principally to our de-spiritualization of life and sweeping embrace of modern materialism. Dawson was relentless in his search to understand why and how we might have arrived at such a critical and detrimental point in the great pilgrimage of the West and mankind.[2]

In order to understand our plight and restore modern culture, Dawson, nearly alone, argued for and demonstrated how a holistic study of culture – including both its spiritual and material aspects – was essential to a truly intelligible knowledge and understanding

---

[2] See for example, Christina Scott, *A Historian and His World: A Life of Christopher Dawson 1889-1970* (London, Sheed and Ward, 1984), and Karl Schmude, *Christopher Dawson: A Biographical Introduction* (Hobart, Tasmania: *The Christopher Dawson Centre for Cultural Studies, 2014).* There is no substitute for a wide reading of Dawson's work as well as that of the many related secondary source considerations of his thought.

of man, and especially modern man. This was the central and unifying theme of nearly all of his work. And the inherent truth of his approach continues to resonate among many of us today.

A crucial aspect of Dawson's thought and holistic approach, as the theme of the colloquium emphasizes, was the notion that such a unitive cultural vision is nearly inimical to the modern academic penchant for disciplinary specialization. Compartmentalization of thought, especially as founded upon a natural science paradigm that eschews the spiritual and intellective dimension of man, vitiates humanistic inquiry. Such an analytical "scientific" and often subjectivist approach was deftly criticized by Dawson in two classic works, in the opening chapters of his exceptional book Progress and Religion (1929), and in The Crisis of Western Education (1961), though his criticism is also implicit in many other of his writings.[3] These two exceptionally synthetic and pivotal works defy summation, for they require what many of lack today, namely, a true liberal educational foundation that facilitates an integrated humanistic and social and natural science interdisciplinary vision.

Instead of attempting to recapitulate Dawson's extensive thought a more efficacious conceptual vantage point will be taken for presenting his vast corpus of ideas. This approach focuses briefly on Dawson's conception of culture, followed by an examination of his notion of the dynamics of cultural change, both of which offer an important introductory key to his overall philosophy of culture

---

[3] Christopher Dawson, *Progress and Religion: An Historical Inquiry*, reprint, 1931, Image Books (Garden City: N.Y., Doubleday, 1960); and Dawson, *The Crisis of Western Education*, With Specific Programs for the Study of Christian Culture by John J. Mulloy (New York: Sheed & Ward, 1961). See also, James Gaston, "The Generative Role of Christianity in Western Culture," *The Crisis of Western Education*, Christopher Dawson, *Humanum: Issues in Family, Culture & Science*, no. two (2015), http://humanumreview.com/articles/christian-culture

and history.[4] This theoretical preparation will prepare the way for a more particularistic though sweeping consideration of the role of migration and diffusion in a liberal educational paradigm, and one focused on the good life as personified in a common integrated cultural way of life.

## The study of culture and the good life

The study of culture and the dynamics of cultural change are essential to Dawson's conception of man's search for the good life. Simply put, man by nature seeks perfection. Every man seeks the good life, though his understanding of the good varies with time and place. The good life, or happiness or excellence, is expressed predominantly in man's religion, in a spiritual vision, though sometimes it is also expressed as a philosophical perspective. At the same time, man is by nature social. He needs others to help him discern the good life. However, equally important, man also needs others to aid him in the pursuit of the particular material goods necessary to the actual living out of his vision. Religion provides the common end toward which men contrive to fashion a common way of social life. This integrated spiritual and material struggle to find, and to live, the good life, constitutes human culture. Dawson argued that only the holistic study of culture provides us with an intelligible understanding of man's vision of the good life, his religion, and the common material social way of life by which he hopes to achieve it.

---

[4] See for example, Dawson, *Dynamics of World History*, ed. John J. Mulloy (London: Sheed and Ward, 1957), for a superlative selection of Dawson essays, as well as Mulloy, *Christianity and the Challenge of History* (Front Royal, VA: Christendom Press, 1995). See also, Gaston, "Christopher Dawson and the Intelligibility of the Integrative Cultural Process", Keynote Address presented at a Colloquium held at Campion College, Sydney, Australia, 31August-2 September 2012, entitled "The Christian View of History and the Revival of the Liberal Arts", *Special Edition, Connor Court Quarterly* 5/6 (December 2012): 137-52.

The holistic study of human culture, therefore, is exceedingly comprehensive, because it must be applicable to all religious visions of the good life and to the multiple social expressions of it. However, human culture must also be considered in light of the near plethora of particular temporal, spatial, social and natural contexts. For this reason Dawson broadly defines culture as the common way of life by which a people adapts themselves to the constraints and possibilities of a place or region. Man's vision of the good life does in fact provide impetus and structure to the common social effort necessary to attain it. Still, man must articulate and adapt his vision of the good life within the contextual milieu in which he finds himself.

But, the element of adaptation also points to the critical notion that culture by its very nature is dynamic, not static. Man is in continuous dialogue with the world. Furthermore, unless a culture remains isolated, such adaptation will likely ensue also in relation to the possible influences of other cultures near or far. In other words, the dynamics of migration and diffusion therefore play a vital role in the formation and continuity – or discontinuity – of nearly every culture. For this reason, given that few if any modern cultures are in fact isolated, the dynamics of migration and diffusion constitute a major element in the contemporary life of human communities.

To state matters in another way, in order to understand ourselves and other cultures, we need to recognize, as Dawson notes, that cultural life through time and space is inspired first and foremost by religion, and this is the key to true human progress and our understanding of it. Modern intellectuals have missed or downplayed this theme due to an excessive concentration on political history, the rise of the centralized state, the birth of the modern nation-state, an overemphasis upon positivist and scientistic analysis, and the relegation of religion to the role of a purely social function void of any true spiritual dimension. Dawson, in contrast, eschews such abstract theory. Instead, he prudently embraces a realistic investigation of culture as a whole.

Such an approach in effect marks the restoration, or perhaps more accurately constitutes the perfection, of a liberal educational perspective. It is liberal in the sense that man's free will, based upon an intellective vision of the good life, constitutes the primary cause of the material cultural expression and development of it. It is educational in that such a holistic perspective honors the truly complex integrated reality of spiritual and material human endeavor. This liberal educational approach facilitates a much more realistic understanding of man, and, in turn, constitutes a genuinely rational pedagogical perspective and method by which to convey, to teach, the wonders and ways of human life.

In comparison, modern specialized approaches to the study of man are overly focused upon the lives of famous or charismatic leaders, the proponents of great ideas, the by-products of political movements and economic conflicts, or the manifestations of deterministic material natural forces and processes. Dawson argues such a truly liberal and holistic cultural approach cuts across all of these philosophies or perspectives and actually unites them, sifts them, and justly interprets them and, hence, man.

The process by which the culture is handed on by the society and acquired by the individual constitutes enculturation. This is a comprehensive process that embraces nearly the totality of human life, and can be studied effectively only by way of an equally holistic approach. This all-encompassing common vision and way of life reveals society's self-identity, as its development and inheritance are actualized in its corporate social life and history. Dawson, therefore, carefully distinguishes education as but a limited and specialized form of enculturation, and one that should not be confused with the truly comprehensive scope of the study of culture as synthetic whole.

Herein one finds the main problem with modern education. It lacks a liberal and holistic cultural perspective because primarily it fails to appreciate fully the role of religion in the formation of culture, and particularly that of Christianity in the development of the West. Modern education has replaced the classical humanist inspired view of man, with a secular humanist vision imbued with utilitarianism, scientific specialization and technology. Such an educational model not only distorts the mind, it also aids and abets the advance of a de-humanized cultural uniformity and standardization in society in general, including the rise of the centralized state. And it does so at the expense of the truly vital and humane local and regional life of the cultures they in fact absorb.

But, as regards our present consideration, the more important aspects of Dawson's notion of culture are two. First, that a culture is a common way of life of a people, and it is composed of a dynamic integration of intellectual and material or biological aspects of reality. The dynamic causal interplay of these elements must be understood if a culture is to be interpreted in an intelligible manner. Second, that it is essential that the culture's tradition, its corporate search for the good life, be conveyed to succeeding generations, otherwise the culture will collapse or be subjugated as its members become alienated from it. Modern secular education is not fitted to such a broad enculturational task because it promotes in its place a limited materialistic and utilitarian vision of the good life. In turn, it has created standardized, nationalistic and globalist, deracinated social way of life, focused primarily on economic production and technological control. This way of life has become our modern heritage.[5]

---

[5] See for example, Dawson, "Vitality and Standardization in Culture", and "Catholicism and the Bourgeois Mind", Mulloy, *Dynamics,* op. cit., 75-79, and 200-230, among many other relevant essays in the same edition.

## The dynamics of culture and the good life

Cultures don't just appear and their integral unity is not static. How do they come about and develop? How do cultures change? Dawson argues that cultures develop and change, that a common way of life arises, as a human group adapts itself to the demands and possibilities of a place or region. The human or geographical milieu presents possibilities for a way of life. But man's religious perspective, or his intellectual acumen or understanding of such a milieu, is the primary cause of his determination of which of the possibilities he ultimately chooses, and how he schemes to survive within the matrix of his localized world. Henceforth, cultural change depends upon successive intellectual or material choices and influences.

However, such possibilities and choices are not endless. There are primary natural occupations which constituted the foundations and future development of all material cultures. They constitute particular types of cultures that seem to embody man's inchoate intellectual capacity to discern, to reason and to form relations with, the material realm. But even these primary cultural expressions are dynamic. Indeed, Dawson's main point is that the history of mankind, its cultural development or change generally conceived, is due not to a single uniform law of progress that posits cultural change "as a continuous and uniform movement", as often implicitly presumed by the modern humanistic educational paradigm. Rather, cultural change is "an exceptional condition, due to a number of distinct causes, which often operate irregularly and spasmodically".[6]

Such distinct causes of cultural change can result from isolated acts of innovation. But much more often they occur as the result of the actual migration of people, the conquering or melding of cultures, or the diffusion of their ideas or their artifacts. People share

---

[6] Dawson, "The Sources of Cultural Change", Mulloy, *Dynamics,* op. cit., 7.

the conceptual and material elements of their culture. In today's global world, cultural change is primarily caused by migration and the concomitant effects associated with the ubiquitous diffusion of ideas, technology and manufactured products.

Regardless of the cause or source, one must recognize, on the one hand, that there is an inherent dynamic quality to any and every culture, due to man's innate never-ending search for reasoned perfection and the good life. And yet, on the other hand, Dawson insists that it is of crucial importance that we recognise that the nature and efficacy of the dynamism of cultural change are dependent primarily upon the intellectual purview of the culture. Cultural change will take place only if, and to the degree that, such potential change is in harmony with the culture's common vision of the good life. Given this dynamic interplay between cultural vision and actual cultural change, Dawson emphasizes that there are five major types of possible historical or cultural change. [7] These types, or genres, are nuanced, and additional qualifications have been added to elucidate them. Still, Dawson has identified the essential aspects, and the point is that each is rooted in the nature of man and culture, and each is related to the dynamics of cultural life and especially migration and diffusion.

First, there is "the simple case of a people that developed its way of life in its original environment without the intrusion of human factors from outside." Here, such cultural change is due to innovation that generally takes place within an isolated milieu. The change consists of a more perfected or more functionally harmonious cultural integration within the isolated matrix of the natural milieu. Once the harmonious relationship ensures basic survival, the culture often remains static, or fundamentally integrated with nature, even for centuries, bar other sporadic

---

[7] Ibid., 7-10. The following quotes that pertain to the five types of cultural change are all drawn from this section of the essay.

innovations. The spatial origin of the innovation constitutes the culture hearth and the source of diffusion. Such innovative change is indicative of primitive "pre-cultures" as Dawson defines them, and is less relevant to this inquiry. However, a broader notion of innovation, one related to the world-wide diffusion of advances in technology, that occur in various global research centers absent any direct relation with the natural regional environment, plays a commanding role in modern cultural change.

Second, there is "the case of a people which comes into a new geographical environment and re-adapts its culture in consequence." In effect, a culture diffuses itself, it moves to a new place, and reintegrates, forms a new common way of life, within the constraints and possibilities of the new local environment. This type of migration is expressed perhaps most clearly in the initial formation of the United States of America and, one could argue, Australia. Colonization in general is a special form of such diffusion or migration, as its purpose and scale is more specialized and limited.

Third, there is "the case of two different peoples, each with its own way of life and social organization, which mixed with one another usually as the result of conquest, occasionally as a result of peaceful contact ... This is the most typical and important of all the causes of culture change, since it sets up an organic process of fusion and change, which transforms both the people and the culture and produces a new cultural entity in a comparatively short space of time." Dawson argues that this process is tripartite. First there comes a period of silent growth. Then there is a period of intense social activity where new forms of culture arise as a result of the vital union of the two previous ways of life. Finally, there is the final period in which the new culture reaches maturity either by absorbing the new elements of the original people, or by attaining a permanent balance between the two, creating a new cultural variation. This process, Dawson argues, also includes the second type, in that spatial and cultural re-adaptation follows at least for one of the two peoples involved. The varying degrees of cultural fusion are expressed in such concepts as acculturation, assimilation, amalgamation and the like. An example of this type of change would be the culture of the American Southwest.

Fourth, there is "the case of a people that adopt some element of material culture which is been developed by another people elsewhere … [but, he notes,] it is remarkable how often such external change leads not to social progress, but to social decay. As a rule, to be progressive change must come from within." This type of change is comparatively superficial to cultural fusion. But it nonetheless can lead to profound social change. There are many classic historical examples of such material expediency, and it abounds in new forms by way of the diffusion of modern technology.

Fifth, there is "the case of the people which modifies its way of life owing to the adoption of new knowledge or beliefs, or some change in its view of life and its conception of reality." In other words, the cultural change is due to the introduction, and acceptance, of new ideas, of new notions of the good life. Furthermore, "The history of mankind, and still more of civilized mankind, shows a continuous process of integration, which, even though it seems to work irregularly, never ceases." This is the most ubiquitous form of cultural change, for, as Dawson notes, "the existence of Reason increases the range of possibilities and the fulfillment of instinctive purpose … For Reason is itself a creative power which is ever organizing the raw material of life and sensible experience into an ordered cosmos of an intelligible world – a world which is not a mere subjective image, but corresponds in a certain measure to the object of reality." The modern world exemplifies this process of cultural change due to its transnational secular humanist conception of man, and its complementary material manifestation and reaffirmation in the industrial and technological order.

As regards the methodical approach or study of such integral cultural change, Dawson emphasized the need to proceed simultaneously in both a synchronic and a diachronic manner. The synchronic approach focuses on the integral character of the culture considering its ideas or vision, its societal expression, its manner of material survival, or work, and its local natural environment in which all of this takes place. A diachronic approach ascertains the key temporal dynamic causes of the culture's change or developmental. In other words, one should employ sociological analysis in order to observe and explicate why and how the intellectual vision motivates a culture to develop the social structures that embody its notion of the good life. And one must also utilise an historical perspective in order to discern which ideas or artifacts are the essential dynamic elements that drive the process of cultural integration and the common way of life. This two-fold approach to the study of culture is truly holistic because it is realistic.

The main point to be made regarding these varied dynamics of cultural change is that they are due to the actual migration or diffusion of people, to the sharing of ideas or artifacts, possibly leading to subjugation or, more often, to some degree of cultural change and synthesis. They are not due to an abstract notion of material "progress" or development. Nor is such cultural change wholly or even predominantly the result of an authoritarian, learned, or intellectual class, or the result of some kind of materialistic determinism or implacable technological order. Rather, cultural change occurs when the society as a whole, imbued with its vision of the good life, forms a common way of life in dynamic relationship with its local cultural or natural environment. The implications of such cultural life and change directly impact the humanities, especially the historical profession, and all the social sciences. Stated succinctly, the way of life of a people is simply, or profoundly, the story of its characteristic cultural change, the historical cultural journey, of a people's enduring search for the good life.

## Western and global culture and the good life

Such then is the theoretical framework or foundation. The argument thus far has been that the search for the good life requires a true liberal educational vision and method holistically focused on the spiritual and material aspects of human culture. This approach must likewise remain cognizant of the directive role of the culture's vision of the good life, and the dynamic role of migration and diffusion in the change and development of its common way of life. An intelligible interpretation of a culture depends upon an authentic explication of society's vision of the good life, and the manner in which the vision provides impetus and structure to a common way of life that embodies its search for the good and useful in all that it does. Still, Dawson emphasizes that the most important and leading cause of cultural life is man's vision of reality. If this is so, then the historical development of a people is an explicative chronicle of its cultural life as lived in and through time and space.

And yet, the permutations of culture and cultural change are not infinite. There are patterns. They arise due chiefly to the nature and limitations of the mind and nature, though they are complicated as they are enriched by the localized factors that characterise a particular place or region. Such patterns can be ascertained, but they rarely present themselves as clearly discrete periods, events or structures. Rather, they are complex integrated cultural ways of life that must be understood.

How should one conceive of a truly interpretive cultural understanding of man past and present? This brings us back to our opening considerations of the importance of liberal education as the basis for our understanding of the good life. Dawson points the way, but his vision is hard to grasp unless one becomes exceedingly familiar with his work and methodological discussions, unless, in other words, one develops such a culturally inspired liberal educational vision for himself.

Therefore, to facilitate such an effort a few brief illustrations are in order. These examples, though sweeping, should exemplify, in a somewhat concrete form, some of the significant patterns of culture and the dynamics of cultural historical change, especially those pertinent to the role of modern migration and diffusion.[8] In the process, the role of a restored liberal educational paradigm in the search for the good life will be reaffirmed, especially in light of the Christian vision of man and life. It is best to proceed by posing and answering some key questions.

First and foremost, what constitutes the good life? Dawson argued that the religious vision of a people constitutes its version of the good life, and its common culture as a whole is in fact imbued with the religion's tenets. As he astutely observed in his Preface to Progress and Religion, "Every living culture must possess some spiritual dynamic which provides the energy necessary for that sustained social effort which is civilization. Normally this dynamic is supplied by religion, but in exceptional circumstances the religious impulse may disguise itself under philosophical or political forms."[9] In light of this quote, there are in effect three types of good life in general, and as revealed particularly in the West.

First, the good life for pre-modern cultures across the globe is solely the result of their religious vision and the manner in which

---

[8] See for example, Gaston, *Steel and the Upper Ohio Valley: A Study in Cultural and Regional Unity*, unpublished paper including maps and pictures, Presented at "Twenty Years of Catholic Studies: A Conference in Honor of Dr Don Briel", University of Mary, Bismarck, ND, 29-31 August 2014 (2014).

[9] Dawson, op. cit., 8.

it informs the life of the primitive cult, the village, and that of the more advanced ancient city-state and empire civilizations.[10] These societies possess a common religion and culture. But their mythopoeic vision of reality, as expressed especially in the religiously autocratic civilizations, lacks that fundamental rational dimension that allows the individual truly to thrive in a dignified manner. They possess a common culture but one in which the good life of the individual is ultimately arrested.

Second, for those societies imbued by "philosophical or political forms", they primarily represent the type of culture which arose with the birth of the modern Western civilization. Its prototype is Greece and Rome. Both embraced philosophic and political forms, many of which are also characteristic of modern civilization. But in the end both implode because their overarching vision of the state alienated the individual as it thwarted that true life-giving localized patriotic way of life so essential to their claims for a vivacious good life.

Ancient Greek culture was diminished as the common cultural way of life of the polis progressively embraced a sophisticated humanism while it simultaneously ceased to maintain its vital relation with its regional hinterland. Rome, in a similar manner, lost the Republic's initial citizen-soldier patriotic fervor as the Empire expanded and embraced multiple religions and cultures. In the end, the common culture of a Pax Romana, which was based upon a philosophically inclusive humanism but in practical terms vacuous Stoicism, or a semi-religious centralised Augustan rule, ultimately left the state the predominant arbiter of the good life. Gone was the local or regional common culture that once engendered the

---

[10] See for example, Dawson, *The Age of the Gods: A Study in the Origins of Culture in Prehistoric Europe and the Ancient Near East*, reprint, 1928, with an introduction by Dermot Quinn, The Works of Christopher Dawson, (Washington, DC: The Catholic University of America Press, 2012), in general, and especially Chapter VI, "The City State and the Development of Sumerian Culture", 81-102.

dignified vital life of the Roman Republican citizen. Migrating barbaric peoples soon conquered the once robust Rome, as they did Greece. In short, the Greeks embraced the citizen but failed to sustain a localized common culture, whereas the Romans fostered a legal and administrative common culture but failed to embrace the localized citizen. Both ultimately relied upon the state to contrive a common though alienated way of life.

The modern version of such statism is characterized by the secular and subjective Calvinist-inspired "bourgeois mind". Its overall penchant for philosophical humanism and political sovereignty results in the creation and control of a common culture inherently beneficial to a primarily materialistic industrial and technological way of life. It is in effect a volatile amalgamation of the ancient civilizations. Its volatility is due to the remnant dynamic moral impulse of the Christian search for perfection and the good life in light of the Eternal. But the Western materialistic technological order, and its global diffusion, lacks the Catholic Christian personal ethical vision and its concomitant moral social constraints. In Dawson's mind modern Communist China may well epitomizes this phenomena, though the transnational focus on technology has become characteristic of many of the modern developing Oriental cultures, and hence, most of the world.[11]

---

[11] See for example, Dawson, *Christianity and the New Age*, reprint, 1931 (Manchester, NH: Sophia Institute Press, 1985). Chinese President Xi Jinping has continually reaffirmed his embrace of economic globalism, referring to it as an irreversible historical trend. To this end, China will continue to adopt policies to promote high standards of liberal trade and investment because the pursuit of economic globalization will make life more inclusive, equitable and beneficial to all, whereas nationalistic economic policies create seclusion that leaves some "behind". See for example, H. E. Xi Jinping, "Keynote speech by Chinese President Xi Jinping at the APEC CEO Summit" (Lima, Peru: 19 November 2016). http://www.globaltimes.cn/content/1019023.shtml, and Jinping, "Full Text of Chinese President Xi's Address at APEC CEO Summit" (Da Nang, Vietnam: 10 November 2017). http://news.xinhuanet.com/english/2017-11/11/c_136743492.htm.

Third, there is a Roman Catholic notion of the good life. The substance of Dawson's work is an examination of the unique qualities of the Christian vision of the good life, and the manner in which its religious and philosophic ideas have become incarnate in the common culture of the West and Europe. His vision of "the making of Europe" simply cannot be adequately recapitulated. But basically he argues that the Christian transcendent and Incarnational vision of the cosmos, resulting in a true notion of the dignity of human person and the goodness and order of creation, bequeaths a spiritually-inspired and rational concept of individual self-perfection and liberty. This eschatology informs and fashions a just and charitable corporate way of life that ultimately becomes prudentially and progressively institutionalized in the vibrant local and regional ethnic European cultures. In time, however, the Christian Medieval way of life is transformed as the *eschaton* becomes immanentised, and the modern world arises.

In other words, the Christian vision and its social realization of the good life attenuate all of the conceptual and structural constraints typical of pagan and materialistic human cultures and societies. It offers a true vision of the common good and the subsidiary manner by which a local common culture can seek to attain it. For the Christian vision proposes a true via media between the spiritual and the material, the individual and the society, and the human cultural and the natural environment. The Christian vision, and the Christian culture that emanates from it, tempers – as far as humanly possible – the inherent tensions in reality including mankind's way of life.

Nevertheless, Dawson reaffirms that a holistic and culturally based liberal educational paradigm is requisite to an intelligent understanding of such Catholic culture(s), as it is for any culture. He poignantly states,

> What we need is not an encyclopedic knowledge of all the products of Christian culture [or any and every culture], but [rather] a study of the culture-process itself from its spiritual and theological roots, through its organic historical growth to its cultural fruits. It is this organic relation between theology, history and culture which provides the integrative principle in Catholic higher education ... "[12]

Moreover, there is the additional Catholic Christian spiritual dimension. The vital principle of the Incarnation imbues the Church and, *mutatis mutandis*, the formation of the individual, who, in turn, plays the generative role in the search to discern and to develop a truly humane and peacefully good way of life. Dawson, in concert with other great Catholic thinkers over the ages, wishes to understand and explicate this vision in a more intelligible manner.

Why is a common culture so important? Because man as a social being cannot perfect himself without the help of others. But the actualization of such perfection can only take place in a communal relationship with the material context or environment in which the culture resides. Therefore, the cultural vision, be it religious, or philosophical or political, and especially Catholic, must and will permeate the common way of life, especially in the formation and development of civilization. In short, a change in the cultural vision will impact the material expression of the culture, just as change in the material aspect must yield a corresponding modification of its religious or intellective vision. A common integrated culture is essential to the maintenance and continuity of any and every good way of life.

Why must the culture be passed on, why is enculturation so important? Because it is essential to the well-being of the individual (and the society) that he understand the cultural vision of the good

---

[12] Dawson, *Crisis*, op. cit., 137-38.

life and partake in the effort to secure it. If such a cultural identity and way of life is not conveyed to the next generation, the culture, as mentioned, will unravel or be conquered. This will result because the individual will be alienated and de-humanized as he does not understand why and how the community seeks the good life. He will fail to participate and perfect himself, and cultural unity and integration will be diminished proportionately. This problem characterizes much of the modern world.

What role does a liberal education play in the continuous search for the good life? As Dawson notes time and again, an intelligible understanding of culture is found only in the broad and holistic act of enculturation. Modern notions of education are focused on much more limited forms of knowledge and activity. However, even more important, in the modern world, a liberal education, properly understood, has almost become a necessity if one is critically to interpret and to assess the false, irrational and undignified focus on the material aspects of reality and the human condition. Elements of such a restored or perfected liberal educational paradigm are the subject of this colloquium.

How does all this apply to the modern world? Dawson's essay on the Bourgeois Mind captures brilliantly the essence of the issue. Ultimately it is a question of religious and intellectual temperament. The modern bourgeois attitude is focused primarily on the quantitative and not the qualitative aspects of reality. It is a way of life rooted in the human natural desire to calculate rather than to love and give of oneself. Dawson summarizes by quoting St Augustine's proclamation that "Two loves built two cities". The modern world has built a social, political, economic city that does not, as St Thomas Aquinas notes, "involve any honorable or necessary end." It is no longer characterized by a Christian eschatological vision and vital Christian agape, but rather by a devotion to nature, material instrumentality, and a respectable average standard, all of which coalesce in a deracinated urban cultural life style. [13]

In the modern world, authority has been transferred from the spiritual and individual realm to that of the humanist sovereign state. In the process the vivacious localized common way of life of small cities and regions has withered. They have been replaced by expansive nation-state civilizations, or the rise of more geographically extensive and culturally inclusive visions of a world society, as represented in the United Nations, the European Union, and the dream a new global order. These entities are bent on the centralized control of an uprooted and amorphous working class that has become bound in urbanized industrial and technological servitude. The vision driving this cultural movement, in tandem with the bourgeois mind, is the modern physico-mathematical model of the sciences, a generic scientism that produces a technologically-based standardized industrial way of life. As a result, the good life has become a life focused on work, ensnared in intra-national and international economic organizations, and reinforced by state-controlled political systems under the guise of "the democratic way of life."

Finally, what role do migration and diffusion play in the modern national and global world? Simply put, both are intrinsic to it. Migration abounds, though the diffusion of the technological order is preeminent. The modern mantra is one that claims the good life of secular cultural diversity. This way of life is enhanced and supported by migration, via transparent or open borders. However, compliance to the worldwide technological vision and order is the dominant principle.

Nonetheless, migration and diffusion both inherently sustain an effete cultural multiplicity incapable of engendering a truly dignified and integral cultural unicity. They help fashion personal

[13] Dawson, "Catholicism and the Bourgeois Mind", Mulloy, *Dynamics,* op. cit., 200-230.

ways of life, dedicated to an apparent and specious individual good, characterized and achieved in a life of production and consumption, and assuaged by ephemeral infatuations with technology and social media. The good life, for the worker and migrant, consists in a mainly unidimensional focus on economic self-survival. But this perspective and way of life steadily generates concomitant cultural tensions at the local, regional and national levels of society. As a result, this pervasive bourgeois attitude reaffirms, by default, a somewhat palatable acceptance of a tolerant social humanism, and the requisite national and global statist authority and power necessary to enculturate it. For differences in religion, culture and language tend to yield culturally unstable aggregations of peoples. And these disparate ways of life, though acknowledged and endorsed, ultimately oblige they be managed and somewhat uniformly controlled.

Modern state-sponsored compulsory education plays a crucial role in the management of such basically diverse human cultural resources. It does so as it progressively replaces the traditional humanistic vision of the good life with a materialistic notion compatible with industrial and technological society. And it provides the attendant practical vocational and technical training preparatory to a functional, though increasingly unendurable, dehumanized culture. The primary agent of modernity is the state, and education is its indispensable partner.

However, the main point to be made is that modern education not only facilitates modern culture, but that, much more importantly, its perspective and method also inherently obscure a true comprehension and assessment of its pedagogy, and thus, that of the culture it in turn helps to create. This is directly related to migration and diffusion given that the modern ersatz cultural fusions of peoples do in fact constitute syntheses of all five types of cultural change as enumerated by Dawson. Modern cultures are tense and dynamically variable admixtures, because the multiple variations of them must be revealed in, and characterized by, their regional possibilities and constraints. Each culture is similar and yet different. And each must be discerned on its own grounds. But the modernist educational vision is incapable of this fundamental act of understanding. It is impotent for all the reasons enumerated and especially due to its failure to consider the human spiritual and intellective dimension of culture.

This brings us back once more to the importance of education as the basis for living the good life. Modern education is essentially flawed. What is needed is a restoration and perfection of the traditional humanistic vision of the good life. And this renewed approach must embrace a truly liberal and holistic cultural perspective, one focused on the essential role of religion in the formation of society, especially that of Christianity, and one that ascertains the real dynamics of cultural formation and change.

The Catholic notion of an ecclesial worldwide spiritual society that honors local life and pietistic practice has been replaced by a globalist vision and social structure. The result is the creation of the prevalent diverse yet ever more materially uniform modern cultures, often extensive urban ethnic manufacturing ghettos, which lack truly good and natural civilized local and regional ways of life. This situation is one of the key elements in the ensuing crisis of the 20th century that Dawson foresaw and lamented.

Nonetheless, it must be remembered that a major exception to this modernist advance has been the British and American cultures. Both are founded on a vision of true human equality, based on a Christian vision of man, and rooted in natural law. And both have institutionalised this vision in political societies that defend, in their respective ways, the liberty of the individual to enculturate this tradition, as he must, in vibrant local communities. Still, this vital heritage is under attack, and it is essential that such a patrimony continue to be articulated and lived.[14]

In closing, it is crucial that we restore a proper notion of liberal education if we are to discern what truly constitutes a good life and comprehend the manner in which it can in fact be lived. Such an effort must be founded on a Christian notion of the dignity of man which embraces an understanding of the necessity of an integrated spiritual and material common way of life. It likewise requires a true appreciation of the nature of culture and cultural change at the local and regional level of society. The Catholic Christian conception of the good life is one of Incarnational peace. And a renewed liberal education will reaffirm our understanding of it, and, in turn, help us prudently ascertain how to live it. Christopher Dawson has reminded us of this essential vision and way of life. We should continue to note well his wise insight and counsel.

---

[14] See for example, Pope Benedict XVI, *Address of His Holiness Benedict XVI to the Bishops of the United States of America on Their "Ad Limina" Visit*, (Rome: Libreria Editrice Vaticana, 2012). Herein Pope Benedict XVI expresses a keen grasp of this crucial subject, especially as it pertains to America.

# 4

## HOW THE POSTMODERN MINDSET IS DESTROYING MODERN MINDS

### *Gary Johns*

By the time children have been taught history was a mistake, and that every piece of classic literature must be torn apart to see what it was like for women, blacks, gays and anyone else who was seen to be a loser, students in the 21st century have no idea how the magnificent society in which they live came to pass. It must seem a complete mystery that anything good has ever come of the world, or that there is such a thing as progress.

I am not well acquainted with school and university curricula in the humanities and social sciences in recent years, but I read enough to judge that many students are fed a diet critical of much that has gone before, just as I was in the 1970s, and in later stints at university.

It is common for lecturers and students to rail against the dominant view of the world. That is as it should be.

The trouble is that too many university lecturers have jumped straight from the grand critique of society, and devotion to a grand plan for a future society, for example Marxism, to another bandwagon – post modernism.

This leap may stem from disappointment among intellectuals at the failure of the "grand designs" or "emancipatory projects" within the modern era for the perfect society, for example Fascism, Marxism, and arguably, more latterly Islam.

As if to hide their disappointment postmodernism offers a salve. At its most theoretical postmodernism suggests that interpretations of reality are contingent on experience and knowledge, which in turn depends on the individuals place in society. Things look different depending on who you are. This insight is not unreasonable and explains why people vote the way they do, even against an objective measure of what is in their own best interests. But, this is the point at which we part ways with the postmodernists. Which is pretty well at the beginning! It is possible, I believe, to prove that someone will be better off under some circumstances rather than other circumstances. The fact that people act on interpretations of reality does not impose an absolute or final limit to knowledge. Because things look different depending on who you are, postmodernism tends to categorise experiences by the identity of those who may not have succeeded in society: female, black, ethnic, gay and so on.

The postmodern analysis (or arguably its misuse in the hands of those who find it suits their purposes) tends to understate the individuals ability to change, or act outside of an identity designation. It also undersells the genius of liberal democracy, which has created freedoms for all, albeit at different paces and to different degrees. The big problem in post modernism arises when identities are thought, or argued, to be permanent, and when policies are based on the permanence of, or even desire to, be different: to exalt in ones identity. Difference becomes the goal, and inclusiveness becomes the policy remedy. First, insist on the right to be different then devise policies to make others accept the difference. Postmodernists argue that too often history is seen as a singular trajectory to something better: call it progress. That may be valid criticism of some versions of history, but progression may look singular in retrospect, but perhaps not at the time. The problem for our intellectuals here is that there is no new "grand design" on offer to compete with liberal democracy (with a strong dash of welfare state).

Which brings us to the other element of postmodernism: disappointment that the "winning design", liberal democracy, is not good for everyone.

The observation has plenty of truth to it, and has led researchers to look afresh at history through the eyes of losers. A variety of allegedly "repressed histories of modernity" such as those of women, homosexuals and the colonised have been written. The purpose of these histories is to lay claim that "modernism" is, or was,

"patriarchal and racist, dominated by white heterosexual men". As a result, one of the most common themes addressed within post-modernism relates to cultural identity. The danger inherent in the postmodern mind is that it starts out grouchy, because it does not have its own grand design, indeed it disdains the idea, because of the disaster of its once feted alternatives, and picks away at the "best design" with the risk that it throws out the baby with the bath water. As someone remarked recently, "there is not a shred of gratitude" for the achievement of the liberal society. Liberty is shown the door, and celebration of difference becomes a glori-ous cul-de-sac. Postmodernism also tends to believe that dialogue across groups is not possible, that is, 'my reality is not your reality', and 'you cannot know what it is like for me', and so on. This belief is acute in the literary world where some are berated for writing about people outside their 'group'. Of course, this silliness is easy to laugh off, but it exists and it is a serious conversation in some university faculties and at many literary conferences.

How depressing.

Postmodernism lacks historical knowledge of, and gratitude for, that which been achieved by mankind.

It fails to appreciate the great achievements in liberty in recent times and underplays the source of liberty, the Enlightenment and its predecessor intellectual endeavours closely associated with Christian theology, and democracy.

It also fails to appreciate the vehicle of liberation, often, white privileged males.

The achievements of liberal society are discounted because of the identity of the achiever.

It mistakes delayed, or uneven shares in progress, for systemic flaws, rather than legacies of earlier cultures and systems. It also fails to account for the persistence of destructive or repressive cultures.

## Egalitarianism

There is also a second string to the postmodern bow: it is closely aligned to egalitarianism. For example, a post modernist may argue that the US was not a completely good society until a black was elected President. The same may have been argued in the UK, until a woman was elected. But, somehow the wrong candidate got up, Margaret Thatcher, and now, heaven forbid, Theresa May, both Tories.

So, there tends to be a bias in the postmodern set that identity works only if it works for another project entirely: the egalitarian project.

I think that the big contest today is between liberty and equality. My value set is that liberty is essential, equality (of outcomes) is not.

Equality depends a great deal on behaviour, and behaviour is to some degree independent of political form.

The chances of attaining liberty (and democracy) depend a great deal on values in a society.

As the economist Paul Collier argues, the transmission of culture from one generation to the next may lock a group, or an entire society into a dysfunctional state.

An aspect of the European cultural transition, and indeed a measure of civilisation, analysed by the psychologist Stephen Pinker (The Better Angels of our Nature), is the decline in violence.

William Pitt the younger was involved in a duel with a fellow MP in 1798, when he was Prime Minister of England! Civilised societies transit "from codes of honour to codes of justice". The transition means that the obligation to avenge a harm passes from the aggrieved family, with the potential for vendettas, to the state.

In some societies, however, this transition has yet to occur.

The anthropologist George Foster suggested that development was frustrated by the belief that interpersonal relations were zero-sum. Recent work suggests that a substantial proportion of the population of the Democratic Republic of the Congo, for example, views interpersonal relationships as zero-sum, privileging witchcraft over effort and luck as the explanation for success. This culture is alive and well in Aboriginal communities in remote Australia.

Then again, some cultures breed success.

The wonderful Deirdre McCloskey, in her book *Bourgeois Dignity: why economics can't explain the modern world*, suggests that the key to the European economic takeoff during "the Bourgeois Era" was the dignity afforded and liberty granted the innovating classes.

McCloskey's thesis explicitly counters the conventional account of progress in terms of the primacy of institutions, getting the rules right, and emphasises the emergent values of a middle class. She sees these new values as foundations for economic transformation.

Nor is inequality proof of failure: inequality is not the enemy.

As the Nobel prize winning economist Angus Deaton points out, inequality is part and parcel of progress.

*The Great Escape: Health, Wealth, and the Origins of Inequality* is the story of progress, cast as "the endless dance between progress and inequality, about how progress creates inequality, and how inequality can sometimes be helpful – showing others the way, or providing incentives for catching up – and sometimes unhelpful — when those who have escaped protect their positions by destroying escape routes behind them".

Only in the latter sense can inequality be said to be harmful.

The rich in Australia have not set out to destroy escape routes by, for example, destroying public schools and hospitals.

As Deaton and Mancur Olson before him argue: "rent-seeking of an ever-growing number of focused interest groups pursuing their own self-interest at the expense of an uncoordinated majority" may harm economic growth.

What leftist acolytes fail to understand is that their supporters may not be so much victims as self-interested.

Difference can be entirely morally based. For example, as Colllier points out, those who are aspirational place a high value on success. Aspirational people choose to work hard. People who work hard vote for low taxes on the returns to effort.

Conversely, non-aspirational people do not work hard and so prefer high taxes on effort. Hence, in a democratic society where taxes reflect majority preferences, there is a critical proportion of aspirational people above which the society adopts low taxes and below which it adopts high taxes – for example, the United States versus Europe, perhaps.

For egalitarians, and probably for post modernists, although for different reasons, such differences are uncomfortable to contemplate.

Trawling for differences, especially difference based on identity, as proof of societal failure may lead to illiberal policies, for example taking more money from people, and ignores the real reasons why some will continue to fail or remain different.

It is important to understand how and why societies changed for the better, especially those societies where all behaviour changed for the better, not just a privileged few. The fact that there may be lagging groups does not serve to prove that progress was not creating opportunities for both leading and lagging groups.

The "Troubled Families Program", launched by the British Government in 2011, for example, "targets a mere 120,000 households that are collectively estimated to have generated £9 billion of public costs". The same results can found in Australia, the same targeting is now on the agenda.

Understanding the behaviour of such households in the conventional rational choice framework of incentives and interests, denies the influence of distinctive values and cultures.

It is time to recognise that culture matters, and that there is no compelling reason to expect these processes to be benign, even in a liberal society.

There is bad behaviour among some groups, and changing morals can help, more so than mere redistribution or taxing the rich.

## William Wilberforce

Postmodernists underplay the value to laggard groups of the changes that stirred society in the great liberal revolution, of which William Wilberforce and the abolition of the slave trade was one.

It is not just about a white, male elite grabbing all of the privileges or extracting the wealth or labour of poor or repressed groups.

I had the good fortune earlier in the year to debate the proposition for the abolition of Section 18C of the Racial Discrimination Act

(Cth) 1975, before a large audience of students at the University of Queensland.

One female student asked me and my fellow abolitionist, Professor James Allen of the UQ law school, why middle aged white men wanted the abolition of a 'protection' against so-called hate speech which, she assumed would only ever be directed at women and other so-called minority's or powerless groups.

We, of course, reminded her that free speech was the greatest protection for any group or individual and that historically middle aged white men were frequently leading voices in the emancipation of oppressed groups.

Had we the time, it would have been worthwhile recounting to her the story of the abolition of the black slave trade, in which blacks, whites and Arabs indulged for centuries: but only middle class white men organised to abolish.

Indeed, civil society activists, of whom I have been critical for their irrational views and imposition on the taxpayer for support of matters that are doubtfully in the 'public interest' often remind me of the great work of church activists in the abolition of slavery.

I agree, but here are the differences they fail to acknowledge.

Wilberforce had the great fortune to be white, heterosexual, wealthy, male, and Christian: not the stuff of modern day heroes. Despite these credentials he did good works.

Wilberforce and his Methodist colleagues used UK legislation in 1807 to abolish the slave trade in the West Indies and beyond. And in a separate Act in 1834, 800,000 [mainly in the West Indies] slaves were set free.

There were economic interests, slave traders and plantation owners in the West Indies who opposed him. Indeed, England compensated slave owners £20 million sterling for ending their immoral acts.

There were economic consequences, but the cause was unambiguously correct – the dignity of freedom.

Not only did William Wilberforce help to abolish the slave trade indulged in by the British, but thanks to the British and its parliament and other institutions much more is known of the black and white slave trade than would have been the case.

For example, the Arab controlled, black and white slave trade, which in some places such as Mauritania and Morocco existed until very recently is denied officially and among many Islamic scholars.

Contemporary scholars of the postmodern persuasion want, no doubt, to be the new saviours, following in the tracks of the abolitionists.

But, they mistake fashion for substance, hoping to be in the vanguard of saving minority's when the minorities are no longer repressed en masse and by law.

A more subtle reading of the influence of culture and behaviour suggest very different policy prescriptions than the current cries for restrictions on free speech a la section 18C, and snarling at white, male privilege.

It is not the slave traders and plantation owners who stand in the way of individual woman, blacks, gays, but programs that suit an egalitarian interpretation of human rights.

Wilberforce in parliament made the great and forceful statement – "Christianity has been called the law of liberty."

Wilberforce achieved not only the emancipation of slaves, he achieved a moral revolution (see Eric Metaxas wonderful account in his book, *Amazing Grace*).

**From abolishing slavery to subsidised free speech**
Wilberforce made doing good fashionable.

Indeed, doing good is now very fashionable …. But is it unambiguously good?

For example, in Wilberforce's time, black slaves returned to Sierra Leone (Freetown), and Haiti was granted its freedom. These experiments to have former slaves establish their own nations did not turn out well, but that was no reason to not grant freedom.

An unassailable moral purpose, such as liberty can afford subsequent failure: liberty means the freedom to fail as well as succeed.

Today, doing good often has a less clear moral purpose, and any downside should be closely scrutinised, because it may not be caused by the liberal society. It is as likely to be caused by the interventions designed to overcome the 'inequality'.

For example, is opposing mining in the third world good and moral? The High Court of Australia thought so.

An Australian charity, Aid/Watch, which did no more charitable deeds than pursue this highly ideological point in its campaigns was held by the High Court of Australia in 2010 (Aid/Watch v the ATO) to be entitled to free speech and therefore be a charity.

I have two problems with this ruling. First, the charity did no charitable work (a point made by justices Heydon and Keiffel) and two, no one inhibited its free speech, indeed, an unwitting public subsidised its 'free' speech.

Is subsidised speech, via the deductible gift recipient status of a charity, free speech?

Is opposing coal mining moral? And yet many environmental charities do so, and are subsidised by the public whose views would be very different.

Why does the public subsidise the free speech of charities that argue less than clear moral cases?

As I point out in my book *The Charity Ball*, a number of

charities have recently argued that they want to return to their Christian purpose, but most of their money comes from a mostly unsuspecting, taxpaying, public, and they do not argue to forsake that money as part of the renewal of their purpose.

Does the tax payer agree with their purpose? Remember, taxation is compulsory, donations are voluntary. Tax deducted donations conflate the two. They actually mean that the taxpayer has a say in your charitable purpose.

In an example that I know only too well, the post-colonial collective self determination dream of Aboriginal identity has cruelled the lives of tens of thousands of Aborigines caught up in the Whiteman's dream of land rights, and public subventions (see my Aboriginal Self-Determination: the Whiteman's Dream)…

Why does the public subsidise such controversial work?

## Conclusion

A final word on good and talented people, as opposed to the collective into which they may, in some people's minds, fit.

Often, determined individuals make the difference. The recent film, Hidden Figures, tells the story of three brilliant African-American women – Katherine Johnson, Dorothy Vaughan and Mary Jackson – who serve at NASA in the 1960s as the brains behind the launch into orbit of astronaut John Glenn.

They, as well as US federal legislation, created freedom for blacks.

Many of the problems of African-Americans are legacy issues, not identity issues, especially the huge rate of single-parent families among African Americans.

The postmodern mind does not have to err to the radical, but it easily fits the urge to criticise all that has gone before, often belittling great achievements and misdiagnosing problems.

As students seek to unravel the parts of history that do not suit them, will they miss the big picture, one part of which is that Christianity and liberty are closely interwoven?

The cynics point to the path to modernity as hell, warring religious and national rivalries and so on, but hell is the retreat from its achievement implicit in post modernism, and its confrere, egalitarianism.

Liberty is more likely to deliver the elimination of prejudice, and more likely to make differences immaterial.

The lesson that I would like to teach students is simple, the identity of the achiever matters not nearly as much as the achievement.

# 5

# LET'S CALL THE WHOLE THING OFF?
## God, Truth, and Buckminster Fuller

*Philippa Martyr*

In this presentation, I want to cover ground that I've never covered before in public, so excuse me if some of this is a bit ragged; I am still working out my position on some of these issues. That's why there is a question mark at the end of my title, because I am not sure whether I really want to call the whole thing off, or not.

John Izzard wrote something quite scathing about people like us back in 2014, in an article in *Quadrant Online* called "Western Civilisation's Weekend Warriors".[1] It was about the IPA's symposium held that year in Melbourne, with Professor Sir Roger Scruton as the keynote speaker. John identified that what has been missing when we all get together like this is a genuine call to arms; some real and practical solutions. He says we need to focus much more on solutions to the problems, rather than just describing the same problems over and over again.

I agree with him, but when I start to think about how we might address the problems in front of us, I very quickly become overwhelmed. The problems in our education system, notably the three Big Wrongs in modern education that have been identified for us to consider this weekend – premature specialisation, loss of a

---

[1] John Izzard, "Western Civilisation's Weekend Warriors", *Quadrant Online,* 12 May 2014, https://quadrant.org.au/opinion/qed/2014/05/western-civilisations-weekend-warriors/ – accessed 8 May 2017.

common culture, and loss of religion – seem to me to be entangled and enmeshed to such a suffocating degree that I really do want to call the whole thing off.

In order for this paper to make sense, I have to start with three observations, all of which are about me. The first is that I am a practising Catholic, and someone who has no problem making that public, because it's an essential part of who I am, and it influences all my thinking. This includes my thinking about the meaning and purpose of liberal education. The older I get, the harder it is for me to argue about liberal ideas from any other angle. I am amazed at people who argue in defence of the liberal arts from a non-Christian perspective. I am thrilled by your audacity: as far as I am concerned, these arguments fall over at the first knock of moral relativism. I believe in moral absolutes, and these shape my approach to liberal ideas. Perhaps that's a contradiction in terms, but I can live with that.

The second thing is: I stand here as part of the problem. I have lived very happily off the public purse for years; first as a university lecturer in Tasmania for six years, and more recently as a public servant in Western Australia for nine years. I still do some university lecturing, in a broadening unit that is designed primarily to make the university money, rather than to improve the world at large. I can offer no defence of my conduct except that I needed the money. But I'm very aware that I could be accused of biting the hand that has fed me so successfully for so long.

My third point is that I recently discovered that I have been evolving into something called a "Catholic libertarian". What on earth is a Catholic libertarian? Libertarianism as a political philosophy, in a nutshell, seeks to limit the role of the State and to maximise personal autonomy. In practice, libertarians are sometimes confused with libertines, because they tend to focus on deregulating the more popular types of mortal sin, and because leftist libertarians are usually advocates of unfettered sexual expression.

If you want to see what libertarianism can look like when it's organised, visit the Liberal Democratic Party's website here in Australia.[2] Their platform includes deregulating tobacco sales, gun ownership, the use of bike helmets, and illegal drugs. They are pro-assisted suicide, which they see as a victimless crime, and they are pro-gay marriage to the extent that they don't think the State has a role in marriage at all, and that the Marriage Act should be repealed, and people should be free to contract whatever types of domestic partnerships they wish.

And yet if you go and read their other policies, there is a surprising amount that a practising Catholic can actually agree with. For example:

- balanced budgets;
- greatly reduced welfare spending, based on the argument that much of our welfare spending is perpetuating poverty, and not alleviating it;
- far lower taxes across the board;
- far greater localisation of government – the LDP take on this is entirely consistent with the Catholic principle of subsidiarity.

They also support the privatisation and/or scrapping of wasteful and inefficient agencies like SBS and the ABC, and bodies like the Human Rights Commission, none of which are friends to the Catholic Church.

So why might there be a problem with being .a Catholic libertarian? It's partly to do with how the Catholic Church has publicly dialogued with the political world: for decades it's been dominated by a socialist and centralist economic line. Some parts

---

[2] http://www.ldp.org.au/ – accessed 7 July 2017.

of the Catholic Church in Australia, for example, have been pretty shameless about encouraging people to vote Labor for years.[3] As Catholics, of course we want issues of social justice to be addressed, but the proposed solutions from within the hierarchy always seemed to boil down to more welfare payments, and more income redistribution, and more government intervention.

But there's plenty in the Church's history and teaching that supports ideas like limited government, free enterprise, legitimate profit, and voluntarism, and all of these are also consistent with economic libertarian thinking. There are also increasingly louder voices within the Church itself trying to stimulate a discussion about this. Catholic libertarianism has been really evolving since the 1980s neoconservative revolution.[4] In this post-Tea Party and current Trump era, more and more Catholic libertarians are coming out of the closet, and it's quite exciting because we're still hammering out exactly what a Catholic libertarian is, or could be.

In terms of an Apostles Creed, I would suggest that all of us believe

---

[3] The historical relationship between the Catholic Church in Australia and the Australian Labor Party is well-known and well-documented. See also Charles Moore, "The Spectator's Notes", *Spectator*, 3 June 2017, 6, for the UK equivalent, where in the recent election, the Catholic bishops appeared to have embraced the UK Liberal-Democratic (Lib-Dem) party platform.

[4] Some basic reading should include Michael Novak's classic 1982 work *The Spirit of Democratic Capitalism*; also Samuel Gregg, *Tea Party Catholic: the Catholic Case for Limited Government, a Free Economy, and Human Flourishing* (Crossroad Publishing Company), which is dull but thorough. John Paul II biographer George Weigel has also been a consistent presenter of the pro-capitalism Catholic world view, to some criticism: Anthony Annett, "The enduring George Weigel problem", *Commonweal*, 28 May 2015, https://www.commonwealmagazine.org/enduring-george-weigel-problem – accessed 4 May 2017. More locally, see Fr Anthony Percy, *Entrepreneurship in the Catholic Tradition*, Lexington Books. For non-Catholics and Catholics alike, Rodney Stark provide a compelling argument for Christian libertarianism. I particularly recommend his *Victory of Reason: how Christianity led to freedom, capitalism and Western success* (Random House).

in smaller government, lower taxes, voluntary charity, and a social framework based on the Ten Commandments.[5] But outside of that, all bets are off: we have Distributists arguing with free market capitalists; we have quasi-mystical eco-anarchists arguing with classical liberal economists, we have a group which I call the 'Optionistas' (those proposing variously the Benedict, Sophia, Patrick, Ignatius, Marian and Dominic Options for saving civilisation),[6] and everything else, and it's all quite lively and enjoyable.

### Is the real problem actually the involvement of the State?

When I approached the Colloquium theme from the angle of a Catholic libertarian, the three Big Wrongs we have identified all seemed to be caused by the same thing: the heavy hand of the State. They are the direct result of State funding and the State's almost complete control of the provision of education in Australia. He

---

[5] There is an intriguing "Summa" on the blog *The Libertarian Catholic*, http://thelibertariancatholic.com/summa-of-the-libertarian-catholic/ – accessed 2 May 2017.

[6] See for example David Russell Mosely's series of reviews on his Patheos blog *Letters from the Edge of Elfland*: "Reviewing Rod Dreher's The Benedict Option Part II: The Benedict Option vs the Radical Catholic Reimagination of Everything AKA the Sophia Option", 5 April 2017, http://www.patheos.com/blogs/elflandletters/2017/04/05/reviewing-rod-drehers-benedict-option-part-ii-benedict-option-vs-radical-catholic-reimagination-everything-aka-sophia-option/; "Reviewing the Benedict Option Part III: The Benedict Option vs the Patrick and the Dominic Options", 26 April 2017, http://www.patheos.com/blogs/elflandletters/2017/04/25/reviewing-benedict-option-part-iii-benedict-option-vs-patrick-dominic-options/; "Reviewing the Benedict Option Part IV: The Benedict Option vs Distributism", 26 April 2017, http://www.patheos.com/blogs/elflandletters/2017/04/26/reviewing-benedict-option-part-iv-benedict-option-vs-distributism/ – all accessed 2 May 2017; Nathan W O'Halloran SJ, "Meet the missionaries who are living the Ignatius Option", *America*, 19 June 2017, https://www.americamagazine.org/faith/2017/06/19/meet-missionaries-who-are-living-ignatius-option – accessed 7 July 2017; Carrie Gress, *The Marian Option: God's solution to a civilization in crisis,* St Benedict Books.

who pays the piper, calls the tune. If the State wants 600 head of engineers this year, then the State must be given that, regardless of how much it causes premature specialisation and narrowness of vision. If the State doesn't think traditional humanistic studies have any value, then the State won't mind them being taken over by postmodernists, as long as enrolments keep going up. And if the State chooses to disregard religion as a public good, then the State will facilitate this, directly or indirectly, in a thousand small and large ways, including through the education system.

When I was working in the university system in the 1990s, I was frequently told that the enemy of the university, and especially of the humanities, was something called "economic rationalism", which to me seemed neither economic nor particularly rational. You can call it utilitarianism if you like, but I think once we peel off the labels, what we are left with is an old-fashioned, unreconstructed, State-run monopoly on the provision of education in Australia. The State is also now serving a homogenised buffet of so-called educational choices across the country, and it's largely junk food.

I'm not an anarchist. I do believe that a limited, well-controlled, democratic, secular state is not a bad thing in itself. But we don't have that kind of secular state in Australia – we have a State which is becoming overtly and increasingly hostile towards traditional Judeo-Christian beliefs and principles. And this should prompt us to engage in an examination of conscience: back in the day when the State chose to uphold principles with which we were comfortable, we were all quite happy with its involvement in the education system. When the State was benevolent towards traditional families, and Christianity, and we had a merit-based educational system, we had no problem with allowing the State to fund education in Australia. We even begged the State for money for our independent

Catholic schools, and we saw the obtaining of this as a major victory.

But the State we are now married to is a very different one from the days of our courtship and honeymoon. We are now trapped in a Faustian bargain: a vicious cycle where increasing failure in education is rewarded with increased State funding. In this light, it's hard for me to think that the proposed loss of funding for Catholic schools under the proposed Gonski 2.0 program is a bad thing.[7] I am more inclined to beg the Catholic school system to run away as fast as it can from this money, because it comes with such very tangled strings attached.

And this is about when I start to wonder if we can actually salvage anything from the whole mess of education provision in Australia. This is where calling the whole thing off, and also Buckminster Fuller, come into it. Fuller is alleged to have said something which I think is very wise, and which is also very pertinent to the challenges we are facing here. The quote has several different versions, but I'll give you the easy one: "In order to change an existing paradigm, you do not struggle to try and change the problematic model. You create a new model and make the old one obsolete."[8]

Alasdair MacIntyre warned us back in 1980 in *After Virtue* of the dangers of trying to "shore up the Roman imperium"[9] – of undertaking our own reverse long march through the institutions, and

---

[7] Matthew Knott, "Revealed: how Gonski 2.0 would rip money from Catholic schools to boost public school spending", *Sydney Morning Herald*, 17 June 2017 – http://www.smh.com.au/federal-politics/political-news/revealed-how-gonski-20-would-rip-money-from-catholic-schools-to-boost-public-school-spending-20170617-gwt5jp.html – accessed 20 June 2017.

[8] The textual origin of this quote remains elusive, even for diehard Fuller fans online.

[9] Cited in Rod Dreher, "The Benedict Option", *Spectator*, 15 April 2017, https://www.spectator.co.uk/2017/04/the-benedict-option/ – accessed 8 May 2017.

trying to drag these back to our way of thinking.[10] I think MacIntyre is correct, and we need to be focusing our energies now on alternative structures and ways of operating. So how can we do this? Rod Dreher, author of *The Benedict Option*, has noted that he left out something very important from his book – a discussion of the role of the political economy in saving civilisation.[11] So my take on the theme of this Colloquium is going to come from precisely that angle: I'm going to look at the three Big Wrongs from a Catholic libertarian perspective, and I'm going to see if that throws up any possible solutions.

- *Vocational training and over-specialisation*

I'm not sure that this one is really a Big Wrong after all, because I believe in vocational training, and I am less concerned about the dangers of over-specialisation. The current remedy is that the university system is selling broadening units which are supposed to counteract this trend, and in some cases demanding that students complete basic degrees before specialisation. I don't see either of these as a solution; it just means that young people enter the workforce burdened with a bigger and bigger debt, some or none of which may ever be paid off.[12]

There's nothing wrong with the idea of broadening units, but the place to deliver these is actually at school. After that, students should be sufficiently broadened to undertake vocational or

---

[10] Cited in Peter J. Leithart, "Breaking with the Imperium", *First Things*, 8 April 2016, https://www.firstthings.com/blogs/leithart/2016/04/breaking-with-the-imperium – accessed 20 June 2017.

[11] "Avoiding the Hive", *Front Porch Republic*, 1 May 2017, http://www.frontporchrepublic.com/2017/05/avoiding-the-hive/ – accessed 2 May 2017.

[12] Jared Owens, "University student HECS debt to explode to $11bn by 2026", *The Australian*, 6 April 2016, http://www.theaustralian.com.au/national-affairs/university-student-hecs-debt-to--explode-to-11bn-by-2026/news-story/7e3384ae4acde6e3b018c2582df321bc – accessed 20 June 2016.

professional training. So why isn't this happening in our schools? I think we all know the answers already.[13] It is also very unlikely that any state government in Australia is going to bite the bullet and undertake the necessary purgation and reform of its education system.

I see two possible ways forward: we can work towards increasing the amount of education we deliver privately; and we can work at the same time towards a deregulated education market in Australia.

At the risk of becoming very unpopular, I am not seeking the survival of the current Catholic education system as part of this process. I think that in most dioceses in Australia, it has now become a de facto cheap private schooling option. That's nice, but it's not what it was set up to do. I have seen good bishops try very hard to reform their local Catholic Education Offices in different parts of Australia for around 30 years now, only to be met with resistance at every level, and outcomes which are very hard to measure objectively.

I have thought for a long time that the most honest option for everyone concerned would be for Catholic schools to be sold off and/or turned into independent, privately-run schools which have no further official or financial relationship with the Catholic Church. I don't think we can save the system we already have. I know it seems drastic, but the money raised from the sale of the schools and land could go towards restarting an alternative, authentically Catholic education system. It would be very small, but it would at least be operated with authentic Catholic principles, and under the direct authority of the local bishop.

---

[13] Stephanie Forrest and Aaron Lane, *Review of the National Curriculum,* Institute of Public Affairs, March 2014, http://www.ipa.org.au/portal/uploads/ IPA_Submission-National_Curriculum_Review-March_2014.pdf – accessed 9 May 2017.

What other ways can we develop the delivery of education privately? We all know about homeschooling, and there is also the option of starting a private school independently. The trouble is that these two alternatives are still controlled by the State. The State also controls the university sector: there are so few private and really independent universities in Australia. Campion College is the standout example here, but it's a struggle for it to break even financially, as we simply don't have a sufficient critical mass of population here.

There is a common theme emerging, which is that it's very hard to create alternatives when the State intrudes on everything. When we look at the Roman Empire, the State fell apart, which created the necessary space for alternatives to grow. It's much harder for us to create this kind of space voluntarily, because it requires the cooperation of the State to do this, and the agreement of the electorate – and the electorate are now used to voting themselves free money. This is the great libertarian paradox: we are the people who want to take over the government in order to leave you alone, and we need the State to roll back its own power.

This means that educational deregulation is very unlikely to happen in Australia, without a really open public discussion that will help to change the current mindset. Deregulation of schools has been introduced to a limited extent in the UK, so we know it's possible, once people really know what's being talked about, and can see how it might benefit them.

- *Neglect of traditional humanistic studies and loss of common culture*

I would say straight off that there is no neglect of traditional humanistic studies in Australia. These are rife, but they're mostly appalling, because they've been hijacked and subverted by – again – a State-funded, State-endorsed, State-approved, and State-rewarded post-modernist academic culture. The answer here is again to stop the State funding.

Have we lost a common culture? I don't know whether we've really lost it completely. I believe there is an identifiable 'mainstream' in Australia, and it's quite a reassuring one. We have not gone as far down the path of social destruction as the UK has, with staggering rates of births out of wedlock and divorce and multiple marriages – Australia's indicators are generally better than those of the UK and US.[14]

Something that often gets left out of these statistics is that family and social breakdown is much more prevalent among low-income communities. This is where you get the greatest number of de facto relationships, multi-generational welfare dependency, unstable housing, and substance abuse. These bring the usual outcomes: poorer physical and mental health, greatly reduced aspirations and opportunities, and increased rates of incarceration. It doesn't matter what colour these people are, or what their religion is: the common factor here is always poverty. And the things that made these people poor in the first place are the things that are keeping them poor.

---

[14] Raheem Kassan, "UK mothers most likely to give birth outside wedlock", *Breitbart.com*, 27 August 2015, http://www.breitbart.com/london/2015/08/27/uk-mothers-most-likely-to-give-birth-outside-wedlock/ – accessed 3 May 2017; OECD Family Database, *Share of births outside marriage,* 2 April 2016, https://www.oecd.org/els/family/SF_2_4_Share_births_outside_marriage.pdf – accessed 11 May 2017; Australian Bureau of Statistics, *Marriages and Divorces in Australia 2015,* http://www.abs.gov.au/ausstats/abs@.nsf/mf/3310.0 – accessed 11 May 2017; Matthew Schimkovitz, "How long does an average marriage last around the world?", http://www.hopesandfears.com/hopes/city/city_index/214133-city-index-marriage-lengths – accessed 11 May 2017; Office for National Statistics, *Divorces in England and Wales: 2014,* https://www.ons.gov.uk/peoplepopulationandcommunity/birthsdeathsandmarriages/divorce/bulletins/divorcesinenglandandwales/2014 – accessed 11 May 2017; Australian Bureau of Statistics, *Marriages and Divorces in Australia 2015,* http://www.abs.gov.au/ausstats/abs@.nsf/mf/3310.0 – accessed 11 May 2017.

This is where Catholic libertarianism really starts to make sense for me. If you really want to restore liberal education as a basis for the good life, a radical place to start would be by alleviating poverty. You could assist this process by further deregulating the employment market, lowering the minimum wage, eliminating income tax at the lowest income levels,[15] and reducing taxes on business owners that currently make it harder for them to employ people, especially young people. You alleviate poverty most effectively through workforce participation.

A liberal education can and should be the basis for living a good life, but it needs to be matched with good economic opportunities. I think if we had a deregulated education market and a deregulated employment market, we could open up a lot more doors to young people from disadvantaged backgrounds. If you add to that a commitment to the use of a common language in English, I think real good could happen. If you can boost workforce participation rates, it's also much easier to restore a common culture. When people have jobs and incomes, they like to try to own property. People who own property are much less likely to be involved in social unrest, and much more likely to develop civic pride and build up their local communities.

So again, it's a hard solution, and that means it's one which is unlikely to be undertaken by any government I can imagine. It would currently be electoral suicide. But again, it would need people to commit to ensuring that these are the issues that become matters for national discussion, rather than, say, gay marriage and koala survival rates.

- *Disregard of religion as a public good*

Where does that leave the third Big Wrong: disregard of religion

---

[15] I am indebted to Professor Stephen Schwartz for pointing out that this particular measure doesn't always have the desired effect on alleviating poverty.

as a public good? The Colloquium flier says that 'Religion is a way of looking at the world and our place in it. Without some understanding of the religious dimension we are cut off from our past.' Three things came to my mind in response to this:

- Is the *principal* role of religion to connect us with our past? I don't think so. I think it's a happy side-effect of having a religion, but it's not the main reason we have it.[16]

- When we talk about religion in the public sphere now, the pitch has been irretrievably queered by the incursion of destructive, radicalised Islam. No one wants that in the public sphere.

- Whose fault is it that religion – and by that I mean Christianity – is now largely excluded from the public sphere? I would argue that it's our fault. We have allowed Christianity to become disregarded as a public good. I don't need to remind anyone of our more public failures as a church, especially recent ones.

This is the hardest one for me to talk about, because I have the bleakest view. We have an increasingly hostile secular State facing us down over questions of freedom of religion, and also freedom of speech.[17] There are in fact three interconnected rights which are under threat in Australia today, which we need to fight for much more vigorously than we have been doing:

- freedom of religion;
- freedom of speech; and
- equality of all citizens under just laws.

We currently have profound dysfunction in many areas of our judiciary and our police forces, as well as the heavy hand of bodies

---

[16] Philippa Martyr, "Letter to a New World Pope II", *Connor Court Quarterly*, 3(7): 13-20.

[17] Gerard Henderson, "The Royal Commission, the media, and the Church", *Quadrant*, July-August 2017, 46-50.

like the Human Rights Commission. Christians and other people of goodwill need to be fighting far harder for all three of these rights, not just for freedom of religion. They should be tapping into those deep liberal education roots and pulling out strong convictions that the Christian tradition is the source of these rights, and that they are all worth defending. I know that sometimes we have our argument hijacked by friendly atheists who are big fans of the Enlightenment, and who see the birth of real freedom in the breaking away from organised religion, but we also need to push back a little more against this, while not alienating our allies.[18]

The solution for me here is also a painfully personal one. It's not about restoring liberal education to teach people what a splendid thing Christianity is. It's showing people what a splendid thing Christianity is by letting it transform our individual lives – not in an inward-looking, cranky, cultish way, but in a genuine, open, joyful and loving way. That's the work of a lifetime, and that's the only way that works. There are no short cuts. We can't legislate this into existence; nor should we try.

This is the hardest one to solve, but again I think it's through rolling back the power of the State, and by creating a more liberal society, that we can best do our work of promoting religion. This is also where Catholic libertarianism makes great sense to me – we used to pray after Mass for the liberty and exaltation of the Church, and that word 'liberty' is an important one. Christianity thrives in a truly free society, and if we want to thrive, we have to fight to ensure our society remains free, or restores its lost freedoms. If we can't or won't fight, or if we fail in this fight – and we may well do – then the creation of alternative structures may mean a return to the catacombs.

---

[18] *Pace* Gary Johns. For another example of this Enlightenment prejudice in action, see the otherwise very readable and enjoyable Nick Cater, *The Lucky Culture and the Rise of an Australian Ruling Class,* HarperCollins, 2013.

## Calling the whole thing off?

So I have proposed some very radical solutions to the three Big Wrongs we're discussing in the Colloquium this year. I think all of these solutions are realistic and workable, but they are all difficult, and they would all be extremely unpopular in the current climate. So I think part of our job may be to help change the climate, and try to get these ideas of smaller government, lower taxes and greater social freedom back on the agenda. Without radical change of this sort, we will continue to operate in a stifling climate of State control, where our alternatives are going to be more like underground movements than open ones.

Rod Dreher and others, including American author Yuval Levin,[19] believe that the way forward is for us to develop our own subcultures, but that these should be both cohesive and attractive. I think this is where many of us can go wrong. We are really good at developing alternative ways of living and teaching and writing and being, but we struggle to make those attractive to other people.

This is what I love about Catholic libertarianism: it's a very broad church and it's very welcoming, and it could also be used to re-capture the emotional ground that has been largely stolen by our enemies. Catholic libertarianism is all about genuine social justice, genuine equality of opportunity, and genuine freedom of choice. It may be a pipe dream, and may never move into the mainstream, but it does offer a philosophy that's both cohesive and attractive.

Can we realistically restore liberal education, religion and a common culture in Australia? Maybe, but I don't think it won't be by taking back the existing structures, which I think are now corrupted beyond repair. But if we are going to try creating alternatives, we must commit to playing a very long game, and remember

---

[19] Yuval Levin, *The Fractured Republic: renewing America's social contract in the age of individualism*, Basic Books, 2016.

that we are probably in the season of the furrow, rather than of the harvest.

St Ambrose, who was no fool, and who was also around at a time of imperial decay, wrote to a fellow bishop: "Therefore, let your words be rivers, clean and limpid, so that in your exhortations you may charm the ears of your people. And by the grace of your words win them over to follow your leadership."[20] This is what we're aiming for: charming the ears of the people, and winning them over to our different ways of living by the grace of our words. Our success or failure will depend on whether we really believe that we have something worth offering. Otherwise we will simply remain Western civilisation's weekend warriors.

---

[20] Roman Catholic Liturgy of the Hours [Divine Office], Office of Readings, St Ambrose, 7 December: Second Reading (Epist. 2:1-2,4-5,7: PL edit. [845,] 879, 881).

# 6

## RECLAIMING WISDOM:

## St Thomas Aquinas and the Integration of Knowledge

### *Paul Morrissey*

After having taught undergraduates for 10 years or so and after a stint as a teacher in high school, I have become somewhat disillusioned with our approach to education. It is basically a truism to say that education today has to be relevant, practical, world best standard, interesting, technologically savvy, student centred, et cetera. These buzz words and fads are in some instances meaningless (student-centred, practical, relevant – to what? To whom?), and in other instances more troubling (technologically savvy). Perhaps the biggest frustration with education today is a lack of an overarching vision, a telos that in previous eras would have been encapsulated with the word, wisdom.

Without an overarching goal, education, at all levels, will remain rather piecemeal. Wisdom, in its classical understanding, is integrative drawing together the disparate areas of knowledge. The pursuit of wisdom does not end with a qualification or a piece of paper; it involves a life long pursuit of learning. Perhaps the greatest exponent of a sapiential approach to learning in the Medieval era was St Thomas Aquinas.

Thomas Aquinas (1225-1274) is called the Common Doctor of the Church. He is also referred to as the Angelic Doctor. Both titles are a nod to his being supremely wise. There is a common misconception of Aquinas however: that he is not in tune with reality and too abstract, that his writings are not for the contemporary Church or contemporary man in that they are devoid of subjective experience and too philosophical. Yet Aquinas was the supreme philosopher of the Middle Ages (Westernising Aristotle and harmonising the intellectual patrimony of the West). Furthermore, philosophy was not his stock-in-trade, his main discipline being theology (his official title was Master of the Sacred Page). He wrote numerous, magnificent commentaries on Sacred Scripture. He was supremely humble (he writes nothing of himself), viewing his writings as "nothing but straw". He is buried in a deconsecrated Church in relative – compared to other great Catholic saints – anonymity. He was a poet, composing some of the most beautiful words to honour the hidden Lord in the Blessed Sacrament. He should be known, or so says one of his principal 20th Century interpreters, Joseph Pieper, by his silence.[1] For Aquinas was struck dumb with wonder at the nature of things, at the wonder of being itself.

After determining some of the key aspects of Aquinas's understanding of wisdom, this paper will look at three themes that may help renew education in a sapiential way: the importance of unity and integration, the connatural way of knowing, and the link between knowing and loving.

### Aquinas on the meaning of wisdom

Before looking more formally at St Thomas's writing on wisdom, let us begin with his little known reflection on why a life dedicated to sapiential knowing is worthwhile:

---

[1] Joseph Pieper, *The Silence of St Thomas – Three Essays*, trans. John Murray, SJ and Daniel O'Connor (Indiana: St Augustine's Press, 1999).

Zeal for wisdom has this privilege that, in pursuing its end, it suffices to itself ... In this the contemplation of wisdom is comparable to a game, for two reasons. First, because a game is enjoyable and the contemplation of wisdom carries with it the highest delight ... Then, because a game is not ordered to something else but to itself, and it finds in itself its own end; we also find this in the enjoyment of wisdom ... But contrary to what occurs in the case of our ordinary enjoyments, about which we anticipate that the least hindrance will bother our joy, sometimes greatly disturb it ... it is in itself that the contemplation of wisdom finds the cause of its delight. It does not suffer, therefore, from any anguish such as when we need to wait for something ... that is why divine wisdom compares its own delight to that of a game: "I rejoiced day after day, playing in his presence." (*Proverbs*, 8:30)[2]

Aquinas takes his basic philosophical definition of wisdom from Aristotle: wisdom is the ability to arrange and to judge, the higher the thing to be arranged and judged the greater the wisdom. He gives the example of the ordering of a building. The one who gives form to the building is called architect and is wiser than the one who constructs the materials. Furthermore, in the ordering of human affairs one is called wise when one directs their acts to a fitting end. Therefore, states St Thomas, the one who considers the highest cause of the universe, God, is most fittingly called wise. He cites Augustine's definition of wisdom as "knowledge of divine things." (*De Trin.*, xii, 14) This wisdom, however, is referring to the highest form of philosophical wisdom. A more precise discussion of wisdom as an intellectual (philosophical) virtue is found in the Prima secundae, where Thomas follows Aristotle's definition of wisdom as an intellectual virtue concerning knowledge that is least

---

[2] Thomas Aquinas, *Expositio libri Boetii de ebdomadibus*, Prologue, as cited and translated by Jean-Pierre Torrell, *Saint Thomas Aquinas: The Person and his Work*, (Washington: CUA, 2005), 69.

knowable to our intellects but most knowable in its own nature (that is, the highest causes).[3]

For St Thomas there are three distinct and irreducible "wisdoms": philosophical, theological (*sacra doctrina*) and Gift (Holy Spirit). The first is metaphysical (philosophical) wisdom, founded on human reason. The second is theological wisdom that comes from Sacred Teaching (*sacra doctrina*), founded on the first and infallible Truth (God) as outlined in canonical Scripture. The third is the wisdom of the Holy Spirit, that is, a knowledge of divine things that comes from the Holy Spirit and not through human reason, a *scientia* that comes via the mode of instinct and the inclination to love. The first and second, although in differing ways, use human concepts and reason. Metaphysical wisdom, the wisdom of the intellect, is perfected by divine Wisdom, which is only arrived at through faith. The second and third have a divine source, although each according to its own way.

**Wisdom and the integration of knowledge**

Aquinas was a great synthesiser of knowledge who understood that truth is symphonic, containing an inherent unity. As a theologian Aquinas saw, like Cardinal Newman, that knowledge of the divine unified all truth. However, knowledge of the "inferior" sciences is important in coming to know divine truth. Aquinas considers this unity at the beginning of the Summa asking: "Is Christian theology (sacra doctrina) a single science?"[4] The affirmative answer that Thomas gives is based on the oneness and simplicity of divine knowledge. The unity of theological wisdom is greater

---

[3] Aquinas, *Summa Theologiae*, I-II, q.57, a.2. For an excellent overview of Aristotle's understanding of knowledge of God as wisdom see, Thomas Joseph White, OP, *Wisdom in the Face of Modernity – A Study in Thomistic Natural Theology*, (Florida: Sapientia Press, 2010), 33-64.

[4] Aquinas, *Summa Theologiae*, I, q.1, a.3.

than philosophical wisdom as the latter has natural divisions while theology "extends to everything."[5] Thus theology, for Thomas, "possessed a more intrinsic unity than philosophy, since the latter admits the innate duality of metaphysics and ethics?"[6] In theology all things are treated under the aspect of God, "either because they are God Himself or because they refer to God as their beginning and end."[7] God is the subject of theological scientia therefore the end which the theologian pursues is not simply an accumulation of objective facts about God, but the living God himself.[8] This means that although theological knowledge treats of different aspects such as creation, salvation, Christ etc., its overarching object remains God who is the source of the intrinsic unity of theology.[9]

St Thomas understands that although there are natural distinctions or differing dimensions (what today we would call disciplines) in theology these should retain an underlying unity. Based on the studies of Jean-Pierre Torrell, we can describe three such dimensions in Thomas's work. First is the speculative dimension, or what is called *intellectus fidei* – to bring one's reason to what is held by faith. Second is his effort to understand (both historically and allegorically), so as to better preach, the sacred Scriptures. This dimension is the most neglected of Thomas's theology. His formal academic title was *Magister in Sacra Pagina* (Master of the Sacred Page) and Scripture was the soul of his theological vision. The third dimension is what Torrell calls the mystical, meaning

---

[5] Ibid.

[6] Servais Pinckaers, OP *The Sources of Christian Ethics*, trans. Sr Mary Thomas Noble OP (Washington DC: Catholic University of America Press, 1995), xxi.

[7] Aquinas, *Summa Theologiae*, I, q.1, a.7.

[8] Jean-Pierre Torrell, "St Thomas Aquinas: Theologian and Mystic," *Nova et Vetera*, English Edition, Vol. 4, No. 1 (2006): 1-16.5.

[9] Aquinas, *Summa Theologiae*, I, q.1, a.7.

how, practically speaking, the Christian returns to God (what today is called moral theology). Louis Bouyer sums up well this unitive dimension:

> Theology, as St Thomas quite expressly understood it, is an organic whole, not artificially and as it were externally unified by an independent philosophy, but proceeding from the inner unity of God's revelation and his whole saving design, a unity which in any case is essentially mysterious.[10]

If theology addresses the overarching wisdom that is God, human wisdom in all its forms must be accounted for on its own terms. Philosophy, the natural sciences, the behavioural sciences, history, exegesis, etc., need to be addressed if theology is to be made incarnate in the world.[11] Only when this occurs can theology fulfil its task of grounding all natural knowledge in its most fundamental dimension. One sees a glimpse of this, for example, in Alasdair MacIntyre's recent work on universities.[12] He argues that modern universities are multiversities where philosophy and especially theology have been eliminated. Reinstating their primacy, at least

---

[10] Louis Bouyer, *The Invisible Father: Approaches to the Mystery of Divinity*, trans. Hugh Gilbert OSB. (Petersham, Massachusetts: St Bede's Publications, 1999), 255.

[11] This is a point made by the Congregation of the Doctrine of Faith in *Donum Veritas: on the Ecclesial Vocation of the Theologian*, www.vatican.va/roman_curia/congregations/, n.10.

[12] Alasdair MacIntyre, *God, Philosophy, Universities: A Selective History of the Catholic Philosophical Tradition* (London: Rowman & Littlefield, 2009). Cardinal Newman's point is relevant here: "Divine truth differs in kind from human, but so do human truths differ in kind from one another. If the knowledge of the Creator is in a different order from knowledge of the creature, so in like manner metaphysical science is in a different order from physical, physics from history, history from ethics. You will soon break up into fragments the whole circle of secular knowledge, if you begin with the mutilation of the divine." John Henry Newman, *Idea of a University*, (Indiana: UNDA, 1982), 19-20.

within a Catholic university, could once again unite disparate faculties in seeking a unified knowledge of all being. A sapiential approach to knowledge would help unite wisdom in its varying forms, especially insofar as it is open to (and can master) the wisdom found outside of theology.

Wisdom is a lost concept today having been replaced by technical knowledge, calculated reasoning, or artistic creativity. There is, Avery Dulles concedes, a wisdom in mastering a particular area, but, "Wisdom in the full and unrestricted sense of the word belongs to those who can discourse about reality in general, seeing all things in their mutual interrelationships, and assigning to each its proper place within an intelligible whole. To be able to perceive the similarities and differences, the mutual dependences and orientations of a vast multitude of distinct realities is a superlative exercise of intellectual power."[13]

Dulles underlines several cultural reasons for the fragmentation of knowledge:

> Democratization, individualism, and the mobility of populations. The ever-accelerating progress of technology has brought different cultures and ideologies into close contact. The slow moving, culturally unified traditional society seems to be a thing of the past. In the current situation it is easy to fall into the historical and cultural relativism and abandon the quest for permanent and universal truth.[14]

Education is fragmented because there is surer footing in a more specialised expertise; any universal knowledge or reality is seen as unattainable.

---

[13] Avery Cardinal Dulles, SJ, "Wisdom as the Source of Unity for Theology," in Michael Dauphinais & Matthew Levering, (eds), *Wisdom and Holiness, Science and Scholarship: Essays in Honor of Matthew L. Lamb*, (Naples, Fl.: Sapientia Press, 2007), 61.

[14] Ibid., 60.

Cardinal Newman saw the importance of a liberal education that unites rather than fragments. A liberally educated student "apprehends the great outlines of knowledge, the principles on which it rests, the scale of its parts, its lights and its shades, its great points and its little, as he otherwise cannot apprehend them. Hence it is that his education is called liberal. A habit of mind is formed which lasts through life, of which the attributes are freedom, equitableness, calmness, moderation, and wisdom, or what in a former discourse I have ventured to call a philosophical habit."[15] Further to the acquiring of professional or vocational knowledge society needs citizens who are liberally minded so as to mitigate against fragmentation.

Society itself requires some other contribution from each individual, besides the particular duties of his profession. And if no such liberal intercourse be established, it is the common failing of human nature, to be engrossed with the petty views and interests, to underrate the importance of all in which we are not concerned and to carry our partial notions into cases where they are inapplicable, to act, in short as so many unconnected units, displacing and repelling each other.[16]

## Connatural knowledge

An essential ingredient of understanding learning as sapiential is Aquinas's teaching on connatural knowledge. This teaching states that an important component of knowledge (really any knowledge) is that which is gained by experience and sympathy. In the practical realm this is obvious: one learns how to change a tyre in a far deeper way by actually changing a tyre than by simply reading about how to change a tyre. Even in more theoretical domains this holds true as well. For example, we learn maths by doing maths;

[15] Newman, op. cit., 76.
[16] Newman, op. cit., 127,128

we also will learn maths in a deeper way if we have a degree of sympathy (affection) for mathematical knowledge. The same holds true, says St Thomas, with theological and moral knowledge. This understanding of knowledge as connatural is something that was lost after the Enlightenment, where to be an intellectual means to be objective, to shut out the passions and experience and to rely solely on reason.

One of the principle ways that St Thomas speaks about connatural knowledge is in the area of virtue. The life of virtue can be compared with the experience of an artist or a tradesman who through repeated experience (even mistakes) will come to know his or her trade in a deeper more intuitive way, leading to a greater freedom. It is the same with virtue. When we repeatedly act in a just way we learn what justice is. The universal concept of justice is thus related to the particular circumstance of moral action. The same applies to all the virtues. The most important recent interpreter of Aquinas's ethics, Servais Pinckaers, OP writes that, "In this work where we encounter reality, both interior and external, we develop a kind of knowledge that is proper to virtue, a knowledge attained through connaturality: a rapid, sure, penetrating, and intuitive ability to judge. We see things at a glance, as skilled and experienced workers do. This kind of knowledge is accompanied by inspiration, which favours invention and creativity."[17]

We should note, however, returning to St Thomas, that connatural knowledge (or wisdom) is different to knowledge derived from the intellect alone. St Thomas elaborates on this point when he speaks about there being two ways of being wise: the first being wise in

---

[17] Pinckaers, "The Role of Virtue in Moral Theology," Servais Pinckaers, OP,"The Role of Virtue in Moral Theology," trans. Mary Thomas Noble, OP in Berman, John & Titus, Craig Steven (eds), *The Pinckaers Reader – Renewing Thomistic Moral Theology* (Washington: Catholic University of America, 2005), 299 (emphasis mine).

a connatural way through the acquired virtue of prudence which accords to the person a sympathy with the good; the second being wise in a cognitive sense having an intellectual knowledge of what is morally good.[18] However, the second kind of wisdom requires the first if the universal is to reach the particular. St Thomas states: As by the habits of natural understanding and science, a man is rightly disposed with regard to general truths, so, in order that he be rightly disposed with regard to the particular principles of action, namely, their ends, he needs to be perfected by certain habits, whereby it becomes, as it were, connatural to him to judge rightly about an end. The virtuous man judges rightly of the end of virtue, because, as Aristotle says in *Ethics* III, "as a man is, so does the end seem to him."[19] Pinckaers gives an excellent synthesis of connatural moral knowledge:

The need for right experience thanks to the experience acquired at the level of intelligence and action, knowledge of morality, itself universal like the laws or norms it studies, can reach its full development through the virtue of prudence, which is personal, and can be transformed into an active, experiential knowledge. Through virtue a kind of reciprocity is established between science and prudence, thought and action, reflection and experience. In a morality based on the virtues, the ethicist cannot remain at a distance from her object, nor can she maintain a kind of neutral attitude toward good and evil. Her personal commitment to the

---

[18] "Since having a formed judgment characterizes the wise person, so there are two kinds of wisdom according to the two ways of passing judgment. This may be arrived at from a natural bent that way, as when a person who possesses the habit of a virtue rightly commits himself to what should be done in consonance with it, because he is already in sympathy with it; hence Aristotle remarks that the virtuous man himself sets the measure and standard for human acts (Ethics, Bk. X). Alternatively, the judgment may be arrived at through a cognitive process, as when a person soundly instructed in moral science can appreciate the activity of virtues he does not himself possess." Aquinas, *Summa Theologiae*, I 1.6 ad3.
[19] Ibid. , I-II 58, 5.

good and the true is needed, lest she be lacking in the experience indispensable for the perception of profound ethical realities.[20]

The rehabilitation of St Thomas's teaching on connatural knowledge is extremely important, especially in the area of ethics. When ethics divides the universal from the particular there exists a permanent state of tension between law (universal) and freedom (the particular). Therefore moral experience cannot unify the two as the theory of connatural knowledge does. Individual experience is not to be trusted or is sometimes termed 'pre-moral.' Therefore, it is assumed today that to study ethics one does not have to be ethical; to study moral theology one does not need to live out the faith. "It even seems," writes Pinckaers, "that the rational exigencies of knowledge demand that the ethicist distinguish clearly between her study and her personal belief or devotion. She may even consider this separation a necessary form of asceticism that will guarantee the objectivity and universality of her research. True moral wisdom, however, must unite the speculative and cognitive with the lived, connatural way of knowing."[21]

## Knowledge and love

Connected to connatural knowledge is the link between knowledge and love. Modernity with its roots in the Enlightenment sought to divorce love and knowledge. This, certainly in the theological sense, is problematic. In Jewish and Christian thought to "know" someone was to love them fully, the two becoming one in the sexual act. Servais Pinckaers notes that a fuller understanding of truth does not just involve ideas but "grows out of a concrete, total experience engaging the entire person in encounter with the other." This, he adds, is really a description of our relation to God.[22] This

---

[20] Pinckaers, "The Role of Virtue in Moral Theology," 301.

[21] Ibid., 299

[22] Pinckaers, The Sources of Christian Ethics, 34.

co-inheres with a classical definition of truth – "the mind's grasp of a thing" – but, adds Pinckaers, with an added something, namely that the thing grasped is not simply a material object but a personal reality – God or neighbour." This personal reality reveals itself in all its nature and mystery as light, goodness, beauty, energy, life. Mind is not now abstract reason but intelligence united to will, love, and desire, informing and directing them. It is understanding joined to sensitivity and imagination, guiding and regulating them."[23] Therefore truth is not merely abstract but involves a person and, furthermore, the intellect having grasped truth is called into action. Thus we are called to live the truth in love. "Truth," states Pinckaers, "is beneficial; through upright love it creates a profound harmony between our various faculties and between persons."[24] This understanding of truth corresponds to St Thomas's definition of the human intellect as "a power that 'reads into' reality (IIaIIae, q 8, aI). It penetrates beyond the outward show of words, gestures, the literal text, to the very depth of a person, a thought, a life, and it understands. This understanding, flowing from active experience and profound contact, gives us a unique kind of knowledge that is universal, constructive, concrete, somewhat intuitive."[25] This knowledge is sure because it is "connatural" being acquired through doing the truth in love. "Its name is wisdom. It culminates in the gift of wisdom, which perfects charity, and the gift of understanding, which perfects faith."[26]

It is essential to "love the truth"; that both love and truth belong together. The French novelist Georges Bernanos wrote about the primordial will to either lie or tell the truth; the determined will to lie will flicker for an instant in the liar's eye revealing the reality of his person. "Love of truth or of lying is primordial, basic to

---

[23] Ibid.

[24] Ibid.

[25] Ibid.

[26] Ibid.

a person, and will affect his actions decisively so that they will be rich or empty."[27] Seeking the fullness of truth – wisdom – is essential in learning. This seeking is an act of the will, an inclining towards a truth that is recognised but not fully grasped.

In his reflection on the epistemological necessity of prayer in understanding Christ, Joseph Ratzinger also highlights the link between loving and knowing. He states a traditional epistemological maxim: "Knowledge depends on a certain similarity between the knower and the known." In personal knowledge this is obvious, we cannot know someone without some empathy so that we "enter into the person or intellectual reality concerned."[28] Ratzinger stresses this point with examples from academia – philosophy can only be acquired if we philosophise; mathematical knowledge will only be acquired if one thinks mathematically etc. The same he adds is true of religious knowledge or truth – and the fundamental act of religion is prayer. This prayer for the Christian is of a specific character: "It is the act of self-surrender by which we enter the Body of Christ. Thus it is an act of love."[29] Previously, in the first of his five theses on the current state of Christology, Ratzinger stressed that the central act of the person of Jesus was prayer, the unbroken eternal communication of love with the Father. Thus to understand or know Jesus we must enter into, participate in, this act of prayer. We must enter into the mind of Christ. Therefore a participation in the mind of Jesus, i.e., in his prayer, which (as we have seen) is an act of love, of self-giving and self-expropriation to men, is not some kind of pious supplement to reading the Gospels, adding nothing to knowledge of him or even being an obstacle to

---

[27] Ibid.

[28] Joseph Cardinal Ratzinger, "Taking Bearings in Christology" in *Behold the Pierced One – An Approach to a Spiritual Christology*, trans. Graham Harrison, (San Francisco: Ignatius, 1986), 25.

[29] Ibid., 26.

the rigorous purity of critical knowing. On the contrary, it is the basic precondition of real understanding, in the sense of modern hermeneutics – i.e., the entering in to the same time and meaning – is to take place.[30] Ratzinger finishes his reflections by stating: "Christology is born of prayer or not at all."[31]

In summary, taking Thomas Aquinas as a guide, we can seek to renew education by taking wisdom as an overarching goal. This means seeking to educate students in an integral way, exploring the interconnectedness of reality and the symphonic nature of truth. Philosophy and Theology play an important role in drawing the reality of the world under the ultimate reality that is God. It also means trying to instill in students a desire to live and to love the true. The life of the mind cannot be separated from the whole of the person. It probably is too noble a goal for our education system today, but may I suggest a motto that would serve us well: To know well, to live well and to love well.

---

[30] Ibid.
[31] Ibid., 46.

# 7

## KAISU: LEARNING COMMUNITIES IN THE SHADOW OF THE INNOVATIVE ECONOMY

### *Julie Rimes*

Perhaps I should begin by giving you something about my own context and what I bring to this colloquium. I am essentially a school teacher. I have been in schools for over 50 years, gaining my first teaching appointment when I was 18 having done my teacher training before that. The school population in the post war era burgeoned beyond expectations and there was a huge demand for people to teach the growing numbers of children of the baby boomers who filled the schools in this state. So the teachers' colleges, two in Tasmania, one in Launceston and one in Hobart, were churning out a new cohort of teachers every six months to supply the growing demand in classrooms.

Our training was very much about methodology, content and practice, with little about the philosophy of education that I can recall. We did have lectures about educational theory, the psychology of learning, and the principles of primary education but little that addressed the notion of education as a basis for living the good life. I stayed in primary education for about thirty years, completed doctoral studies and stayed in schools but worked in the secondary years, the post-secondary years, and as a consultant to predominantly K-12 schools. So this is my context. And what I am going to talk about is the context that surround schools today, that is, the world that we live in, and the schools that prepare people to live in this world. I have taken as my title, "Learning communities in the shadow of the innovative economy' as an invitation to explore how schools seek to provide an education for a good future and a good life.

While I was considering what to present today I was drawn to the opening lines of Dickens' classic novel, *A Tale of Two Cities*, which I first read when I was at school. The opening phrase seems to provide an apt summation in the context of today's world where we have such evidence of the transformation in epochs, wealth, inequality and other elements of our world. You will recall that it is one of the world's classic openers:

> It was the best of times, it was the worst of times, it was the age of wisdom, it was the age of foolishness, it was the epoch of belief, it was the epoch of incredulity, it was the season of Light, it was the season of Darkness, it was the spring of hope, it was the winter of despair ... we had nothing before us, we were all going direct to Heaven, we were all going direct the other way ...

We might also add to this by saying that we live in an age of paradox. Charles Handy referenced this in 1994 in his book, *The Age of Paradox*.[1] Writing at about the same time Andy Hargreaves,[2] the Canadian educator, took up this theme and described five paradoxes with direct implications for educators, and although it was over 20 years ago, it seems relevant still to me. He posited that:

1. "Many parents have given up responsibility for the very things they want schools to stress";
2. "Business often fails to use the skills that it demands schools produce";
3. ironically "more globalism produces more tribalism";

[1] C. Handy (1994). *The Age of Paradox*. Cambridge, Mass.: Harvard Business Press.
[2] A. Hargreaves (1995). "Renewal in the Age of Paradox", *Educational Leadership*. April 1995, Vol. 52, Number 7, 14-19.

4. when there is "More diversity and integration [it] is accompanied by more emphasis on common standards and specialization"; and

5. "Stronger orientation to the future creates greater nostalgia for the past."[2]

All these paradoxes are still enacted in schools today, even though the discourse used to describe these in 2017 has changed. I read an amusing aphorism recently: "There are two things wrong with our schools – everything our children don't learn in them, and everything they do learn."

But continuing on with the theme of paradoxes, some of the paradoxes, or polar opposites, of our times are the magnificent triumphs in technology, and science, and engineering juxtaposed against rather depressing realities of our world. Consider the first Global Future 2045 Congress met in Moscow in 2012 as an example. There, over 50 world leading scientists from multiple disciplines met to develop a strategy for the future development of humankind.

One of the main goals of the Congress was to construct a global network of scientists to further research on the development of cybernetic technology, with the ultimate goal of transferring a human's individual consciousness to an artificial carrier. Is this, I wonder, the dawn of a new era, the era of neohumanity? Currently, we have access to a plethora of such wonderful, at times frightening, projections of how science is shaping and reshaping the world. And some terrifying doomsday predictions as well.

A few weeks ago, I wanted to attend a lecture at the Royal Society in Hobart, but as it clashed with something else, I consoled myself with reading some of the speaker's writing. Barry Brook is an ARC Australian Laureate Professor and Chair of Environmental Sustainability at the University of Tasmania, so his writing is not to be taken lightly. He and another colleague Bradshaw, contributed a refereed paper to the proceedings of the National Academy of Sciences of United States of America in 2014.[3] The abstract reads:

The inexorable demographic momentum of the global human population is rapidly eroding Earth's life-support system. There are consequently more frequent calls to address environmental problems by advocating further reductions in human fertility. To examine how quickly this could lead to a smaller human population, we used scenario-based matrix modelling to project the global population to the year 2100. Assuming a continuation of current trends in mortality reduction, even a rapid transition to a worldwide one child policy leads to a population similar to today's by 2100. Even a catastrophic mass mortality event of 2 billion deaths over a hypothetical 5-y window in the mid-21st century would still yield around 8.5 billion people by 2100. In the absence of catastrophe or large fertility reductions (to fewer than two children per female worldwide), the greatest threats to ecosystems – as measured by regional projections within the 35 global Biodiversity Hotspots – indicate that Africa and South Asia will experience the greatest human pressures on future ecosystems. Humanity's large demographic momentum means that there are no easy policy levers to change the size of the human population substantially over coming decades, short of extreme rapid reductions in female fertility; it will take centuries, and the long-term target remains unclear. However, some reductions could be achieved by mid-century and lead to hundreds of millions fewer people to feed. More immediate results for sustainability would

---

[3] C.J.A. Bradshaw and B.W. Brook (2014). Human population is not a quick fix for environmental problems, National Academy of Sciences of the United States of America. Proceedings, 111, (44) 16610-15515. ISSN 0027-8424.

emerge from policies and technologies that reverse rising consumption of natural resources."[3]

I have five young grandchildren, all of whom I expect and trust will be alive in the year 2100. I fear for them if these scenarios are played out.

I wonder what our world will be like – how will we react, grieve, manage a mass mortality event of two billion deaths? The same applies for "a global one child policy" – how will we react, respond, interpret this? So in view of some of these evidences of the best of times and the worst of times, it is small wonder that one of the most popular movements in schools is the teaching of positivity. Also unsurprisingly, is the fact that one of the very popular literature genre for young people, but not exclusively amongst the young, is dystropic literature. Stating the obvious, one article I read noted:

> The rising popularity of dystopian literature among adolescent audiences is prominent in today's pop culture due to its relevance in young adult's lives, its direct comparisons to current events in today's world ...[4,5]

Margaret Atwood's *The Handmaid's Tale* is enjoying enormous popularity, in book form, stage versions, film, serialised for television, even a ballet.

I think if we reflect back on the first six months of this year we can all bring to mind elements of each of these contrasts – Dickens' words "the epoch of incredulity, the winter of despair, the age of foolishness, and at the same time, the age of wisdom

---

[4] The Artifice (n.d.). The Rising Popularity of Dystopian Literature. Retrieved from https://the-artifice.com/popularity-of-dystopian-literature/ on 27 June 2017.

[5] L. Bradley (2017) The Handmaiden's Tale: How a 30-year-old story became 2017's most vital series. *Vanity Fair*, April 25 2017 Retrieved from, http://www.vanityfair.com/hollywood/2017/04/handmaids-tale-hulu-margaret-atwood-samira-wiley-interview on 22 June 2017.

and light, and hope".[6] As the news continues to be louder, meaner, more violent, more confusing, more divisive, and more heartbreaking, so much so that there is an increasing trend in Australia for parents to delay their viewing of the evening news until after their children have gone to bed for fear of inducing their offspring into night terrors,[7] I have found myself wondering two things, how do these times shape our young people, their thoughts and values and future hopes, and secondly I puzzle over the problem of what is it that education needs to 'be' for us as a basis for 'living the good life'. Thus I was thinking about the characteristics of our world, our culture and the people in it to see what education should be.

There are many words circulating, largely via social media, which seek to define young people. There are described as Millennials, Gen Y, Gen Z, Gen Me, and a new one I heard the other day was Phigital – this is a term referencing the first generation to be unwilling or unable to draw a distinction between the physical world and its digital equivalent.[8] We have all read about these students and their characteristics. The most disturbing insight was a recent comprehensive survey that concluded that the biggest fear of the Millennials is not global terrorism or climate change, or some anthropogenic calamity but in actual fact the lack of wi-fi coverage. Typically, they are described as confident, self-expressive, liberal, upbeat and receptive to new ideas and ways of living, and less positively as materialistic and self-absorbed. Another descriptor I liked, perhaps because it rings true to me, is Kiasu.

---

[6] C. Dickens C., *A Tale of Two Cities*, 1859.
[7] Parenting. (2017). Why you shouldn't watch TV news with your child. Retrieved from http://www.parenting.com/article/tv-news-too-violent-for-children on 18 June 2017.
[8] Education dive. (n.d.) Phigital-students demand new approaches from educators. Retrieved June 26 2017, from http://www.educationdive.com/news/phigital-students-demand-new-approaches-from-educators/444088/

Kiasu is one of those new words making inroads into the English language. It is used prolifically in Singapore, the land of the great PISA results, but it originates in China and refers to a fretful, egoistic mind-set that is petrified of 'missing out'. It is, in fact synonymous with the more English-friendly acronym of FOMO – Fear Of_Missing_Out.[9] Wikipedia defines it as: "a pervasive apprehension that others might be having rewarding experiences from which one is absent".[6] This social angst is characterised by "a desire to stay continually connected with what others are doing".[6] FOMO is also defined as a fear of regret which may lead to a compulsive concern that one might miss an opportunity for social interaction,[10] a novel experience, profitable investment or other satisfying events. In other words, FOMO perpetuates the fear of having made the wrong decision on how to spend time, as "you can imagine how things could be different".[6] And the fear of missing out links directly into the paradox of choice. Too many choices in life don't make us happier, but as the psychologist Barry Schwartz suggests, "choice has made us not freer but more paralyzed, not happier but more dissatisfied".[11] I see this frequently amongst our school leavers, overwhelmed with the choices that seemingly lie before them, fearsome of 'missing out' or making the wrong choice, they agonise over what their next step will be.

So if these are some of the manifestations of the societal mindframe of young Australians, how can learning communities prepare the workers, citizens and leaders of tomorrow? What sort of learning communities are we, in this post-truth Information Age that

[9] FoMO – Fear of Missing Out. (n.d.) Wikipedia. Retrieved from https://en.wikipedia.org/wiki/Fear_of_missing_out 26 June 2017.
[10] Social Interaction. (n.d) Wikipedia. Retrieved from https://en.wikipedia.org/wiki/Social_interaction 26 June 2017.
[11] B. Schwartz (2005). The Paradox of Choice. TedTalk February 2005. Retrieved from, https://www.ted.com/talks/barry_schwartz_on_the_paradox_of_choice on 22 June 2017.

has been characterised as both the age of narcissism and the age of discontinuity, are we bold enough to create?

But before we look into the innovative future it is worthwhile casting our gaze into the past. The famous political philosopher, Machiavelli advised:

> Whoever wishes to foresee the future must consult the past; for human events ever resemble those of preceding times. This arises from the fact that they are produced by men who ever have been, and ever shall be, animated by the same passions, and thus they necessarily have the same results.[12]

> In antiquity, students of a certain class and gender, that is privileged and male, who wished to make a difference in their world had to be well-versed in arithmetic, geometry, music and astronomy, the four subjects that made up the quadrivium.[13]

There were three other additional requirements or prerequisite subjects. The trivium was the lower division of the seven liberal arts, and comprised grammar, logic, and rhetoric. Preparing students to become good citizens and workers seemed easier. They needed to master the mechanics of language, the intricacies of thought and analysis and to apply their mastery of rhetoric so that they appeared wise!

Wisdom of course, does not stop with the ancients. There have been many attempts to define exactly what it is that schooling should achieve for society. Committees and think-tanks abound. I think you will recall the Finn Review which commenced in 1988 and resulted in the Finn Committee competencies in 1991 – viz. Language and Communication, Using Mathematics, Scientific and Technological Understanding, Problem Solving, Personal

---

[12] N. Machiavelli, *The Prince*, 1532.

[13] "Quadrivium", *New International Encyclopedia*, https://en.wikipedia.org/wiki/New_International_Encyclopedia (1st ed.). New York: Dodd, Mead.

and interpersonal and Cultural understanding. Then later in 1992, another business group, this time led by Eric Mayer produced a list of seven key competencies which were seen to build on the Finn competencies: Expressing Ideas and Information, Communication, Collecting, Analysing and Organising Ideas and Information, Using Mathematical Ideas and Techniques, Using Technology, Working with Others and in Teams, and Planning and Organising Activities. And then the Chamber of Commerce and Industry and Business Council had another go at employability skills in 2002 and came up with Communication, Technology, Problem Solving, Teamwork, Planning and Organising, Self-management, Learning Initiative and Enterprise.

These lists of competencies and skills and the work behind them show that debate about what are now often referred to as 21st century skills began in Australia before the end of the 20th century. There have been similar discussions in other parts of the world as well and there have also been significant international efforts to define the skills. Take for example the OECD's 2003 *Key Competencies for a Successful Life and a Well-Functioning Society* edited by Dominique S. Rychen and Laura H. Salganik.[14] This interdisciplinary and international study set out to determine what competencies we need for an overall successful life and a well-functioning society. They decided that interacting in socially heterogeneous groups, acting autonomously, and using tools interactively are indispensable prerequisites for an individually successful life and for sustainable socio-economic and democratic development of society.

I would also like to explore a more recent manifestation of the trivium and the quadrivium of the liberal arts in antiquity, that is, both the Australian Curriculum, and a set of 21st century skills

---

[14] D.S. Rychen and L.H. Salganik (2003) (1st Ed.) *Key Competencies for a Successful Life and a Well-Functioning Society*, OECD, Hogrefe Publishing.

defined in the Cisco, Intel, and Microsoft project led by Australian academics Patrick Griffin, Barry McGaw and Esther Care in 2012.[15] First to the 21st century skills, where again, three major international technology companies, Cisco, Intel, and Microsoft, took the view that, if business and industry wanted educators to pay attention to particular competencies, it was important to define them clearly and to establish how they might be measured. An international team reviewed many sets of definitions and chose not to rule on any one in favour of the others but rather to develop a more general classification into which the various definitions might fit. These categories were "Ways of thinking" to include creativity and innovation, critical thinking, problem solving and decision-making, learning to learn and metacognition. Then "Ways of working" to include communication, collaboration and teamwork. Then "Tools for working" both Information literacy and ICT literacy. And the fourth category "Living in the world" to include Citizenship – global and local.

But what do these categories do for us as teachers in schools? Do they help us decide what we are to teach, or how to teach, and do we care enough to actually unpack them and make them useful for practitioners in schools? How do these categories affect us in schools as we seek to help people lead meaningful, ethical and successful lives? I suspect, rather like the Finn, Mayer, and the 2002 Chamber of Commerce and Industry and Business Council competencies, for those of us at the chalk face, very little. Since the conclusion of the *Assessment and Teaching of 21st Century Skills* project in 2012, some inroads have been made into schools and tertiary institutions but these have mostly involved the traditional gate-keepers, that is, government policy-makers, different education systems as well as the various assessment authorities

---

[15] P. Griffin, B. McGaw and E. Care (eds.) (2012), *Assessment and Teaching of 21st Century Skills*, Springer Publishing Company. New York, NY.

across Australia. I cannot speak of Finland and Singapore, where this project also took place, but in Australia we are loath to break the nexus between the traditional 19th century pen and paper examination that still defines the way we acknowledge, judge and celebrate academic success.

I alluded earlier to the Australian Curriculum as a very central and defining element of what education in Australia is all about. I feel somewhat reticent to go into too much detail, given the company I am in, with due acknowledgement to Dr Donnelly, but it is a discipline-based set of expectations of what all Australian students should be taught, regardless of where they live, or their background. All students from Foundation to Year 10 have access to the same content, and their achievement can be judged against consistent national achievement standards. But the key question is, is it designed to deliver, as Dr Donnelly wrote in his letter to then Education Minister Pyne, "or is so far delivering, what students need, parents expect, and the nation requires"[16] of an education system. Or is it as Wiltshire and Donnelly assert a "monolithic, inflexible and unwieldy curriculum". It sure is! Like the parson's egg – it is good in parts.

But this still does not lead us closer to how do we foster motivated, dedicated learners and prepare them to overcome the unforeseen challenges of tomorrow? One core problem in education is that routine cognitive skills, those that are easiest to teach and easiest to test, are also the skills that are easiest to digitise, automate and outsource. Of course will still need state of the art skills in key disciplines, but success is less about reproducing content knowledge, and more about extrapolating from what we know to apply it to something new, in novel situations. Andreas

---

[16] Commonwealth of Australia (2014) Review of the Australian Curriculum. Final Report. Retrieved from https://docs.education.gov.au/system/files/doc/other/review_of_the_national_curriculum_final_report.pdf on 26 June 2017.

Schleicher at the OECD's Education Directorate summarised it
in 2012:

> Education today is more about ways of thinking which in-
> volve creative and critical approaches to problem-solving
> and decision making. It is also about ways of working,
> including communication and collaboration, as well as
> the tools they require, such as the capacity to recognise
> and exploit the potential of new technologies, or indeed,
> to avert their risk. And last but not least, education is about
> the capacity to live in a multi-faceted world as an active
> and engaged citizen.[17]

Having travelled back in time I would like to change gear now
and speed right ahead into the future and present you with some
thoughts of what a refreshed framework of desirable skills might
look like for the Millennial generation and for the new Information
age. Like the quadrivium and the trivium from antiquity this new
system, also includes seven intersecting realms. Here I propose
that the new seven intersecting realms of Systemic Thinking, Deep
Expertise, Expert Project Management, Complex Problem Solving,
Diversification, Technological Proficiency and becoming a Writing
Worker will form the basis for living the good life in the 21st
century.

Dr Justin Marquis from Online Universities proposes and, in
so doing, acknowledges sources such as *Reinventing Schools: It's
Time to Break the Mold* by Charles M. Reigeluth and Jennifer R.
Karnopp[18] and the project I referenced earlier, the *Assessment and*

---

[17] A. Schleicher (2012). *The case for 21st century learning*. OECD Education
Directorate. Retrieved from Retrieved from http://www.oecd.org/general/
thecasefor21st-centurylearning.htm on 17 June 2017.

[18] C.M. Reigeluth and J.R. Karnopp (2013), *Reinventing Schools: It's Time
to Break the Mold*, Rowman & Littlefield Education. Lanham, Maryland.
USA.

*Teaching of 21st Century Skills* as influential sources.[19] Thus he is following and extending my argument.

Let me just reference briefly what some of these areas of learning and thinking might look like.

Firstly, systemic thinking. Many leading thinkers in the field including Michael Goodman and Art Kleiner highlight the importance of a holistic approach when it comes to learning and providing solutions. Essentially, you cannot address one aspect of education, or learning, or business without impacting on others. This holistic approach to learning and problem solving that has found favour in many disciplines, including medicine, is referred to by most theoreticians as systemic thinking. More than at any time in history, the new information age that we are currently living in, is structured in complex and intersecting systems including educational, political, socio-cultural, economic, technical and institutional ones such as trade union, the church and, of course, the fourth estate, as the enemy of the people, as some loud tweeter-obsessed septuagenarian across the ditch would have us believe.

When an interconnected conglomerate such as Google wants to introduce a new innovation into its business it must rely on systemic thinking to hypothesise how a singular action can impact on others. It should come as no surprise then, that the search engine giant Google has spent has spent over two and a half million dollars to launch a massive crisis campaign in the wake of US President Donald Trump's immigration ban.

I think this example from February this year illustrates two important things:

a) to ensure that you arrive at the best possible outcome,

<hr/>

[19] J. Marquis (2013), Building the Ideal Skill Set for 21st century employment. Accessed on 19 June 2017 http://www.onlineuniversities.com/blog/2013/07/building-the-ideal-skill-set-for-21st-century-employment/

any decision, no matter how controversial or mundane should only be taken after evaluating all the available factors; and

b) the linear thinking that has traditionally been associated with business acumen and success is on the decline. As Michael Goodman and Richard Karash[20] insist that learning, that is, any type of learning, is a cycle, not a linear configuration with a once-through process with a beginning and an end.

Jerome Bruner's writings on the Spiral Curriculum of the 1960s was a game changer in educational theory. Like Piaget, Jerome Bruner believed that children construct knowledge internally by engaging in discovery learning, selecting and transforming information, constructing hypotheses and making decisions. As children grow then, Bruner believed, curriculum should revisit earlier learned ideas, expanding on them until a child reaches a more complete understanding of individual ideas and how they relate to each other. Bruner called this a spiral curriculum wherein ideas are presented in repeated learning from the simple to the complex from the general to the specific, and are examined in relation to one another. You can see here the beginnings of systems thinking approaches although the term would be derived not by Bruner. Systems thinking has roots in a diverse range of sources, in Jan Smuts' holism in the 1920s, to the general systems theory advanced by Ludwig von Bertalanffy in the 1940s and captured cleverly by Peter Senge in his popular book, *The Fifth Discipline*.[21]

---

[20] M. Goodman and R. Kavash (1995), "Going Deeper: Moving from Understanding to Action", *Systems Thinker*, Vol. 6, No. 9. Six Steps to Thinking Systemically. Retrieved from http://www.appliedsystemsthinking.com/supporting_documents/PracticeGoingDeeper.pdf on 22 June 2017.
[21] P. Senge, *The Fifth Discipline*, Random House, 1990.

Fritjof Capra[22] states in his executive summary for his *Life and Leadership* seminars: In this new economy, the processing of information and creation of knowledge are the main sources of productivity. Thus knowledge management, intellectual capital, and organisational learning have become important new concepts in management theory. Applying the systems view of life to organisational learning enables us to clarify the conditions under which learning and knowledge creation take place and to derive important guidelines for the management of today's knowledge-oriented organisations. Systemic thinking acknowledges that the world is complex. One challenge of systemic thinking is that future educators, and especially education leaders, will need to shake off the linear mould of problem solving or strategic planning in dealing with life events. A life event is more than a single episodic experience but includes the factors associated with an experience.

The second essential competency of the 21st century relates to deep expertise. Much bombast and heraldry has accompanied the release of the new HSC in NSW in February this year. According to the chair of the NSW Education Standards Authority, Tony Alegounarias, the new courses in English, Mathematics, Science and History will be characterised by "greater depth, rigour, and mastery of content learning."[23]

Criticising State curricula has admittedly become something of a national past-time in Australia. The renown Michelle Simmons, professor of the Centre for Quantum Computation and Communication Technology at the UNSW, put the cat among the

---

[22] F. Capra (2002). 'Life and leadership: A systems approach. Management seminars.' Retrieved June 25, 2017, from http://www.fritjofcapra.net/summary.html

[23] N. Robinson and R. Armitage (2017) New South Wales HSC syllabus gets overhaul with more complex topics. *ABC News* on 21 February 2017. Retrieved from http://www.abc.net.au/news/2017-02-21/nsw-hsc-syllabus-gets-radical-overhaul-year-12-teaching-changes/8288000 on 20 June 2017.

pigeons, sixteen years ago, when she denounced the role of context associated with scientific formulae and knowledge and it appears that context has since been demonised as a postmodern affectation, or affliction if you like, of all senior curricula. I happen to think an evaluation of context in the Humanities is an imperative. Its appreciation, and the associative empathy and sympathy that results from such cognizance is, I believe, one of the hallmarks of a civilised society. It is not a coincidence, after all, that most medical degrees, across much of Australia, my own state of Tasmania sadly being an exception, are only available as postgraduate degrees in the hope that future medical practitioners will not only be brilliant at diagnosing and curing illnesses but might also employ a systems approach derived from deep learning to their practice to assist the healing process and cure illness.

Countries, geographically close to us, such as China and Singapore, are also in the process of revising their curricula in the hope of providing their students with a deeper, expert understanding of mathematics and science instead of historical practices such as rote-learning which, incidentally, has not served them too badly in the PISA tests.

I'm not advocating for a second the dumbing-down of standards in schools, universities and society. I am an ardent supporter of deep expertise when this is applied judiciously in a given scenario.

Developing deep expertise is not something that's aim is simply to help young Australians do well as school and succeed in securing a place in tertiary institutions. It is about the acquisition of a mindset that values rigorous thinking and hard work and preparing one for skills which are still emerging. Many commentators are asserting that 65% of millennial children entering primary schools in the 2010s will end up working in jobs which have not been invented yet. So one curriculum response has been to focus enormous attention on STEM skills and coding skills. While I have to say that the coding response is a rather late acknowledgment that after 30 years of equipping schools with computers in order to meet the needs of the digital revolution, most computers in schools are used as word processors and information retrieval units, however I endorse the skilling in technology and science whole-heartedly, but note that in addition to specialised technical and communicative skills we must equip students with cognitive and non-cognitive skills. The best way for young people to do this is to avoid early specialisation whilst in high school and study a broad base of subjects which will enable their elastic brain to train itself to respond to different forms of challenges. Deep expertise in any field prepares the template in the brain for becoming expert in other fields as well. As the world gets smaller through globalisation, innovation and economics it is impossible to know how different fields, and subjects will intersect.

The third essential 21st century skill is self-directed learning. It requires young people to not only embrace their own learning but to also become responsible for it. Self-direction in one's learning assumes many forms and countless schools have embraced this both in the delivery of curriculum as well as in their marketing. In Tasmanian schools, an excellent pre-tertiary subject exists, Student Directed Inquiry, whose sole purpose as the title suggests, is to teach self-direct learning through an inquiry approach. I taught this subject for many years and currently work as a Chief Examiner for the subject. It incorporates all the elements that I have been proposing as essential skills for the future. Justin Marquis from Online Universities proposes that the level of change that is occurring at every strata of society is so dizzying that workers need to be self-reliant in finding creative and innovating ways of working. What this means in reality is that the old-fashioned way of professional learning or development that was centralised is already a thing of the past and working professionals need to be proactive in equipping themselves with the essential set of skills that will enable them to carry out their work. As part of a competitive job market employers will always favour workers who can demonstrate a unique set of skills that they bring to the workplace. The multinational consultancy firm McKinsey is just one firm that values employees who are problem solvers, and creative thinkers. They are adamant that successful professionals are ones who are self-directed in their approach and learning and those who can demonstrate a 'personal impact'.

It should come as no surprise that the fourth valued 21st century skill relates to complex problem solving. The pace of change and innovation that is taking place in the global economy and job-market necessitates future workers to be innovative in their approach to problem-solving. But finding solutions for complex problems does not happen in isolation and well-paid leaders in the field will need to guide clients to appreciate that solutions to their hard problems and implementing these solutions will often come at a huge emotional and social cost. Again, finding workable and clever solutions to complex problems requires a strong intellectual ability and a certain expertise in what can be achievable. Such solutions to emerging complex problems will require future workers to delve into diverse areas of expertise such as marketing, ICT, economics, media design, sociology and psychology as well as the core disciplines.

So how can schools prepare students to forge their way in becoming complex problem-solvers? This is not as difficult as it appears. People who will be able to solve complex problems even those that are not as yet manifest are those people who demonstrate a strong academic performance and strong analytical skills. In my view, these are the students who assume leadership positions and are able to execute these well through their effective communication. These are the young people who incorporate work into their school routines (outside homework and assignments), whether this is paid employment or volunteer work, or work through an internship. In addition, the liberal education tradition is a sure fire method to produce innovative thinkers. While it seems odd to reference innovation with what is often thought of as an archaic model, an academic career of last resort, in fact it is a sound pathway to foster innovative thinking. Liberal arts or liberal education? For our purposes here I will suggest that a liberal education is a broad-based study of many disciplines, with an emphasis on inquiry, analysis, and critical thinking. Marquis goes further and suggests that a liberal arts education must cultivate written and oral communication skills, embed some civic engagement across the curriculum, include a foundation in ethical thinking and focus on imparting skills and the curiosity necessary for lifelong learning.[24]

The fifth element of my revised framework concerns diversification. Essentially, it is important as a learner to show some initiative in your learning, and personalise your own pathway. Many of us have been able to create our own career pathway and to follow or develop our passions, and it is never too young to start this. Seeking out alternative ways of adding value to your learning, taking a job or an internship, learning new and quite different skills all have value. Thus diversifying our skill set and our knowledge will become increasingly important. And the sixth subset – having technological proficiency is absolutely essential. While technology may not be everyone's cup of tea it is an undeniable factor in our future. And those having some well-developed hi-tech skills will be those who are able through technology to lead innovation and value add to their career and life. Writer and analyst from ICAS,

---

[24] J. Marquis (2011). "The challenge of crafting a Liberal Arts Education for the Online Learner." Online University Org Blog of 11 September 2011. Retrieved from http://www.onlineuniversities.com/blog/2011/09/the-challenge-of-crafting-a-liberal-arts-education-for-the-online-learner/ on 22 June 2017.

the international body for chartered accountants, Eleanor O'Neill writing late in 2016 noted that the LinkedIn Global Top Skills of 2016 report showed a major demand for technical skills in the workplace with digital knowledge and understanding making up the entire top 10. Employers are reportedly looking more and more to hire experts in data analysis, web design and software development, according to the hiring and recruiting activity that has happened on the LinkedIn professional networking site this year.[25]

So far I have focused on a range of 21st century skill areas that are commonly referenced in a variety of publications internationally. My final offering is one that Roslyn Petelin refers to as being a working writer.[26] Petelin distinguishes between working writers such as journalists, novelists, technical writers and so on, and the writing workers, those workers where a strong writing ability is essential to their working lives, say for example, lawyers, scientists, and researchers and so on. Such writers may not consider themselves a writer by profession, but they find that they become one by default. In my experience, it is the skills of a writing worker that will be a distinguishing feature of our evolving world scene. Knowing how words work, how sentences and form-class words work, how structure-class words and paragraphs work, how punctuation and structure and design work to contribute to meaning are going to be a desirable and an increasingly scarce commodity. It is often only when there is a document-related crisis that the political complexity and sensitivity of different documents becomes exposed and leads to problems of credibility and exposure to risk. Again, alas, there is a declining skill level amongst teachers

---

[25] E. O'Neill (2016), "The Top 10 Skills for professionals in the future," *ICAS*, 1 November 2016. Retrieved from https://www.icas.com/ca-today-news/10-skills-you-need-for-the-future on 22 June 2017.
[26] R. Petelin (2016), *How Writing Works: A Field Guide to Effective Writing*, Allen and Unwin, Crows Nest, NSW.

able to teach good writing skills, and amongst our school teaching force, there is a marked diminution of these skills.

As I indicated earlier, many people are working to bring frameworks of these interrelated skill areas together to have an impact on schools. I am encouraged somewhat that a recent initiative with the Tasmanian Department of Education called *MyEducation*[27] which is being rolled out this year in all government schools seems to share similar aims – albeit under the guise of career education. I have some reservations about this, but this is not the forum in which to air these concerns. Nevertheless, it does apply systemic thinking and approaches, focus on problem solving, and seek to meet the needs of individual learners. We will have to wait and see how it rolls out.

I was intrigued quite recently listening to an interview with British writer David Goodhart. In his book, *The Road to Somewhere: The Populist Revolt and the Future of Politics*, Goodhart[28] describes the characteristics of what he defines as new cultural fault lines in Britain, between what he categorises as the "anywheres", the "somewheres" and the "in-betweeners". Goodhart has divided the world, as he sees it, into "anywheres", that is, citizens of the world, and "somewheres", people who are inherently more socially conservative and more likely to live close to where they grew up, and without putting too fine a point on it, dissatisfied and, with few options for advancement, they are defined as a group belonging to particular places. I will leave aside any debate about whether this is an apt and useful discussion. Nevertheless, if we are to consider the notion of liberal education and what we mean by using education

---

[27] Education Department of Tasmania. (2017), *MyEducation*. Tasmanian Government. Retrieved 26 June 2017, from https://my.education.tas.gov.au/Pages/default.aspx

[28] D. Goodhart (2017), *The Road to Somewhere: The Populist Revolt and the Future of Politics*, Hurst Publishers, London, UK.

as the basis for living the good life then we have these disparate groups to bear in mind. Let me draw on David Goodhart's keynote presentation to the NECE[29] an intellectual think tank involving a broad variety of international experts with different and controversial perspectives based in Europe created as a European and international platform for stakeholders of civil society, scholars and citizenship educators. Speaking of contemporary society in Britain, in particular, but in reference to many Western countries, Goodhart argues:

> What lies behind this political upheaval in most Western countries is a value divergence. The old divides of class and economic interest have not disappeared but are increasingly over-laid by a larger and looser one – between the people who see the world from Anywhere and the people who see it from Somewhere. Anywheres dominate our culture and society. They tend to do well at school – they have been called the "exam-passing classes" – then usually move from home to a residential university (at least in the UK) in their late teens and on to a career in the professions that might take them to London or even abroad for a year or two. Such people have portable "achieved" identities, based on educational and career success which makes them generally comfortable and confident with new places and people. The Somewhere people are by definition more rooted and usually have "ascribed" identities – Scottish farmer, working class Geordie, Cornish housewife – based on group belonging and particular places, which is why they often find rapid change more unsettling. One core group of Somewheres have been called the "left behind" – mainly older white working class men with little education. They have lost economically with the decline of well paid jobs for people without qualifications and culturally,

[29] D. Goodhart (2016), "Crossing Borders, Migration and Citizenship Education". Keynote address Networking European Citizenship Conference 2016.

too, with the disappearance of a distinct working-class culture and the marginalisation of their views in the public conversation. However Somewhere ambivalence about recent social trends spreads far beyond this group and is shared by many in all social classes, especially the least mobile. Despite recent increases in geographical mobility, about 60 per cent of British people still live within 20 miles of where they lived when they were 14.

If we consider our education systems in Australia with the state of vocational education and apprenticeship provision, and the push towards an expanded and graduate-dominated society where educational success is the gold standard of social esteem then it raises questions about the loss of status and respect for those who do not succeed in schools and tertiary education. It is a situation that is particularly telling in relation to Tasmanian educational outcomes. I acknowledge that we live in a world that is defined by the knowledge, and the need to generate new knowledge but I do also acknowledge that, again as we see clearly in Tasmania, not all knowledge and innovation is derived from universities or university graduates. Now, I have spent my working life motivating students to think of themselves as having the skills to work anywhere, and largely they seem to have become 'anywhere' young women. Frequently as teachers we marvel at the interesting careers and achievements of our former students. But it does leave a very large majority of people who are not in this group, and who will not experience a life that satisfies them, sometimes does not even satisfy their basic needs.

So what must be done? What can be done? This question is exercising a lot of minds in Tasmania and elsewhere. People often ask me this same question and I am not entirely sure I have an answer. It is one of the core challenges of our time, to create an educational agenda that will help people lead meaningful, ethical and successful lives. I'm paraphrasing Albert Einstein here when he says, "Data is not information, information is not knowledge, knowledge is not understanding, understanding is not wisdom." We have a lot of information, we have a good deal of knowledge and understanding, but now we need to apply the wisdom of Solomon to help us determine how we frame an education that fits our purpose. I have proposed a new model of seven intersecting realms: Systemic Thinking, Deep Expertise, Expert Project Management, Complex Problem Solving, Diversification, Technological Proficiency and a Writing Worker as a model for a fit for purpose education.

I conclude my deliberations with reference to a recent Australian Council for Educational Leaders (Queensland) statement from which I paraphrase. I acknowledge that I am a member of a profession that extends to me the opportunity and the privilege to make a positive difference in the lives of young people. As I teacher I seek to offer a spirit of optimism, resilience and hope as I support young people to develop and act on the values, beliefs and capabilities that guide them throughout their lives. I accept the responsibilities of being a teacher, and acknowledge the deep trust placed in me by society. In writing this paper I recognise and respect the theory and knowledge which is gifted to me by those who have come before me, as I draw from it and strive to contribute further to it by these thoughts.[30]

---

[30] Australian Council for Educational Leaders. (2017). A Statement of Commitment to the Teaching Profession. ACEL Queensland, 7 April 2017.

# 8

## The Future of Learning: the Role of the Independent Scholar

### *Karl Schmude*

In 1951, the namesake of this important Centre in Hobart, Christopher Dawson, received a special award, the Christian Culture Award, from a Canadian university in Ontario. His acceptance speech was called "Ploughing a Lone Furrow," and he drew attention to the tradition of private, independent study which he himself had followed, and which characterised English research and writing in the past so that it complemented the work of professional historians.

Dawson noted that "there is no longer any room for this tradition in the modern world, where modern methods of co-ordinated research combine with social and economic conditions to make it impossible." He confessed that, if in his lifetime he had had to follow his own line of studies and "plough a lone furrow," it was not out of choice or because he could dispense with the help of other scholars, but because the subject to which he had devoted himself, the study of Christian culture, had no place in modern university studies.[1]

I would like to focus in this paper on three things – first, to sketch the contribution of the independent scholar to the world of learning in the past, and more broadly to the world of culture; secondly,

---

[1] Christopher Dawson, "Ploughing a Lone Furrow," *Christianity and Culture*, ed. by J. Stanley Murphy, Helicon Press, 1960, 17.

to reflect on changes in university and academic life that have affected the capacity, and even the existence, of the independent scholar; and thirdly, to highlight the potential for independent scholarship in present-day culture, given that the university has now come to dominate the world of learning, and even of vocational training. I will be concentrating on recent centuries, particularly from the 18th century, when various scholars were working and writing outside of universities: towering figures such as Samuel Johnson and Edward Gibbon in the 18th century and Charles Darwin in the 19th, who were influenced by their Christian upbringing, even if they later disavowed it, and scholars of Jewish background, such as Karl Marx in the 19th century and Sigmund Freud in the 20th.

In addition to these prominent figures, there was a second – and substantial – rank of writers and thinkers who would have carried the conventional title of "man of letters." Evelyn Waugh once described his father as a "man of letters," and noted that this category was "now almost extinct," like that of the maiden aunt.[2] A fascinating study by John Gross on the man of letters revealed how this distinctive cultural figure emerged in the 19th century as a literary scholar, and was later transmuted into an author in general, particularly in literature.[3] The 19th and early 20th centuries were the age of this sort of independent scholar, who combined literary composition and criticism with practical journalism and writing for a wider public. One thinks of such cultural critics as Thomas Carlyle and Matthew Arnold and Sir John Squire, or, at an even more popular level, writers like G.K. Chesterton (who, despite seeing himself as never more than a journalist, produced, in the midst of his vast output, some acclaimed works of literary criticism,

---

[2] Evelyn Waugh, *A Little Learning,* Chapman & Hall, 1964, 72.
[3] John Gross, *The Rise and Fall of the Man of Letters: Aspects of English Literary Life Since 1800*, Weidenfeld & Nicolson, 1969.

particularly on Charles Dickens, as well as a penetrating study of *The Victorian Age in Literature*).

The term, "public intellectuals," could today be applied to such writers, but this might convey a misleading idea of the cultural purpose which the man of letters served, and his role in the broad dissemination of learning and the shaping of communal understanding. As John Gross notes, in the past most English critics were fortified by the idea that they were the guardians and interpreters of one of the world's great literary traditions.[4] Such a notion, that of being the guardian of a tradition and seeing traditions as at once nourishing and sustaining in the life of a culture, would strike contemporary elites as not just quaint but outrageously wrong-headed, given the prevailing scepticism and even disgust that many seem to have for the traditions and values of Western civilisation. It is somewhat reminiscent of the description by John Ruskin, the 19th century art critic, of the entire output of Fleet Street, the centre of British journalism at that time. Ruskin referred to this output as "so many square leagues of dirtily printed falsehood."[5] Some might think that little has changed in the hurly burly world of journalism today.

More recently, in the 20th century, there have been some notable scholars whose works, often popular in their readership, earned academic respect as well: historians such as Lewis Mumford, an acknowledged authority on cities, and Barbara Tuchman, winner of two Pulitzer Prizes for books on World War I and American-China relations in wartime; and literary figures like Edmund Wilson and Paul Goodman. These independent scholars had no regular academic posts, and often no university connection at all. They were, in the main, independent like Christopher Dawson, whose only academic appointments were, in his early years, at Exeter Univer-

[4] Ibid., 289.
[5] Ibid., 26.

sity, and in his closing years, at Harvard when he was appointed as the inaugural Professor of Catholic Studies in the Harvard Divinity School.

As an independent scholar, Dawson himself contributed to historical understanding with pioneering works of scholarship and analysis. In 1932, for example, he published *The Making of Europe*, perhaps his best-known book, a work of ground-breaking importance. It focused on the Dark Ages as a period of silent growth that paved the way for the extraordinary cultural flowering of the 12th and 13th centuries, a flowering that could not have occurred without this long period of painful, and unappreciated, preparation. Dawson probed the roots and the runners beneath the soil of the society. He saw, below the surface chaos, a creative process at work – the germination of a new way of life, a new Christian culture. He challenged the prevailing view of the Dark Ages, conditioned as it was by the rationalist Enlightenment, and expressed by Voltaire who believed that the Dark Ages presented the historian with "the barren prospect of a thousand years of stupidity and barbarism," by comparison with the creations of the 13th century which "vindicate the greatness of the human spirit."[6] Dawson's singular achievement was to show how these two periods of human history – what Dawson himself called "the long winter of the Dark Ages",[7] on the one hand, and the cultural spring of the 12th and 13th centuries, on the other – were profoundly connected; not a simple black and white contrast, as if the renaissance of the 12th and 13th centuries had come out of nowhere.

*The Making of Europe* was the product of years of quiet research and private reflection on Dawson's part – the devotion

---

[6] Quoted by Christopher Dawson, *The Formation of Christendom*, Sheed & Ward, 1967, 219.

[7] Christina Scott, *A Historian and His World: A Life of Christopher Dawson 1889-1970*, Sheed & Ward, 1984, 103.

of the individual, independent scholar. Despite his reservations about scholarly isolation, which I noted at the outset, the freedom that Dawson enjoyed, both intellectually and in the time and scope it gave him for concentrated work, played a decisive part in the originality of his perspectives – in two respects: first, it heightened his ability to penetrate the inner life of our culture and not merely recognise and record its external manifestations; and secondly, it gave him a greater capacity for synthesis, for bringing together ideas and insights in a way that academic specialisation now forbids. The independent scholar can strive for an integration of knowledge and a coherent worldview that are much harder to achieve in a present-day university setting.

Dawson's analysis in *The Making of Europe* covered both the West and the East. He explored in a seminal way three crucial forces which had been underrated in the shaping of the civilisation of the West – first, the contribution of the barbarian peoples of Northern Europe, which provided its popular grounding, and the wellspring of its native, and later, national loyalties; secondly, the extent to which the universal spread and spirit of citizenship of Rome ("civis Romanus sum") anticipated and prepared for the missionary outreach of the new Christian religion, which stressed a common spiritual citizenship that united all human beings, regardless of geography or race or sex or station in life; and thirdly, the way in which the different threads of cultural life – the Greek and Roman traditions, intellectual, social, institutional and organisational, and the contributions of the barbarian peoples – were brought together by the spiritual dynamism and direction of the Catholic Church, and forged into a cultural synthesis that found supreme expression in new philosophical, educational, artistic, and political forms, such as Aquinas's medieval philosophical synthesis, the birth of the university, the building of the Gothic cathedrals, and the early and embryonic examples of parliamentary government.

In addition to these insights about Western civilisation, Dawson gave serious attention to the East – to the rise of Byzantine culture that contributed to the character of medieval culture and the emergence of Islam and expansion of Muslim culture. Again he revealed an independent view that challenged the received scholarship of the time, notably expressed by Edward Gibbon. This view saw the culture of the East as essentially "a decadent survival from the classical past," which deserved to be denigrated or at least dismissed. Dawson focused on the special strengths of Byzantine culture, which were in the realm of religion and art; but he also looked sympathetically at the political and social strengths of the Eastern Empire. He argued that the prevailing historical view about the Byzantine culture of the East was that it had only been viewed in secular terms, as an economic and political entity. As he noted:

> The modern European is accustomed to look on society as essentially concerned with the present life, and with material needs, and on religion as an influence on the moral life of the individual. But to the Byzantine, and indeed to medieval man in general, the primary society was the religious one, and economic and secular affairs were a secondary consideration.[8]

The independent scholar represented by Christopher Dawson and others has now all but vanished. This reflects not just a loss of independence, for independence is not an end in itself since it has an ultimate purpose, which is to foster the freedom to explore, and finally to embrace, the truth.

Occasionally the independent scholar still pops up in newspapers and magazines. One thinks, for example, of the Australian journalists Paul Kelly and Greg Sheridan, who venture at times outside their designated domain of politics and foreign affairs to

---

[8] Christopher Dawson, *The Making of Europe: An Introduction to the History of European Unity*, Sheed & Ward, 1932, 85-86.

reflect on issues of culture, religion and education; or Peter Craven, a highly knowledgeable literary critic, who writes frequently for a popular audience and not just academic journals.

Another variant of the modern independent scholar is one who has intermittent links with universities, occasionally as a writer-in-residence, such as Australia's "poet-laureate," Les Murray; or the American literary critic Joseph Pearce, who has written biographies of Tolkien, Chesterton, Belloc and others. There are also the refugees from universities, like the British philosopher Roger Scruton, who regards himself as no longer academically respectable and employable and yet continues to be a prolific writer in spite of – or perhaps because of – his self-imposed scholarly exile. There are also those who qualify as independent scholars – indeed, as "men of letters" – who have managed to be freelance writers most of their working life, such as the British author Piers Paul Read. Read is primarily a novelist, but he has also written authoritative histories and biographies, as well as a best-selling account of the survivors of a plane crash in the Andes in the 1970s, *Alive*. But such specimens are now few and far between.

An important mark of the passing of the independent scholar is the virtual disappearance of the academic eccentric, the eccentric scholar within universities as well as outside them. I entered universities in the early 1970s and it was still possible to find the academic eccentric at that time – an individual who was distinctive, irredeemably untidy, incurably absent-minded, and peerlessly unself-conscious. Indeed, that was part of the definition of the eccentric, that he thought everyone else was unusual, not himself. Only in 2016, for example, the Oxford historian, Professor James Campbell, died. He was renowned – if that is the word – for being an absent-minded professor; such as lighting his pipe and then, a few moments later, placing it in his pocket!

If we go back to the 19th century, we recall another Oxford

don, the famously eccentric Dr William Spooner, who became renowned for his "Spoonerisms," of transposing the first letter of two words; as when he knocked on the door of the Dean's office and enquired: "Is the bean dizzy?" Or when he reprimanded a student in these terms: "You have hissed all my mystery lectures" [when he thought he had said "missed all my history lectures"]. "You were caught fighting a liar in the quad" ["lighting a fire"], and "having tasted two worms" [for "wasted two terms"], you will leave by "the next town drain" [actually "the next down train," from Oxford to London].

Apart from his wonderful muddling of words, Spooner also displayed a legendary absent-mindedness, as when he invited an Oxford don to tea, to welcome Stanley Casson, "our new archaeology fellow." "But sir," the man replied, "I am Stanley Casson." "Never mind," Spooner said, "Come all the same."

In the 20th century, one of the most endearing of eccentric scholars was Sir John Squire. He was a poet, critic and founding editor of the journal, *London Mercury*, which showed a distinct boldness in providing an outlet for new writers. Squire had a strong influence on British culture outside of universities, as an independent voice, in opposing literary modernism between the World Wars, for which he earned the scorn of writers like Virginia Woolf and T.S. Eliot.

Squire was also an historian, but his approach was unconventional – the mark of an independent scholar. This was shown by his interest in historical speculation. He thought that conjecturing about the past – of asking questions beginning with "if", or "suppose", or "if only" – was not at odds with what had actually happened. Rather it offered new ways of reflecting on the past, and fostered intuitive understanding and insight. His interest in historical conjectures led him to edit a collection of essays of "alternative history", called *If It Had Happened Otherwise* (1931). In this work, various contributors speculated on the course of history if certain events had turned out differently. Thus, G.K. Chesterton wondered if Don John of Austria had married Mary Queen of Scots, thereby extinguishing Scottish Calvinism and, by serving jointly on the English throne, arrested the Reformation and kept England a Catholic country. Squire himself contemplated the impact on English literature if, in 1930, it had been discovered that Bacon really did write Shakespeare.

No doubt these now sound simply facetious and frivolous, but such conjectures can be illuminating. They provoke the imagination to look at alternatives, and probe the inner and underlying realities of history, not just the outward manifestations; the inner substance, not just the external evidence. They can help to counter the claim, often heard nowadays, that supporting a new and fashionable cause will ensure we end up "on the right side of history," as if history is predestined and predictable, when it is so plainly unpredictable and seemingly arbitrary (except for those who, as Christians believe, discern in the unfolding of history a divine meaning and a providential purpose). The independent scholar is less likely to be seduced by such a notion as being "on the right side of history," recognising that it injects a false and self-serving authority into any debate, and can be too easily enlisted in support of favoured social and political movements, such as the current same-sex marriage debate, which should rely on substantive arguments, not spurious historical summons.

Many of the stories about academic eccentrics may be apocryphal, but even so, the fact that they seem believable, and have often been retold, resonates with the need for the scholar to cultivate a certain detachment from the consuming concerns of everyday experience. In G.K. Chesterton's famous comment, absence of mind is really only the presence of mind on something else. The point about the absent-minded professor is that he was absorbed in his own world of learning, undistracted by competing interests or the trivia of everyday life. In particular, he was largely immune to the insinuations of conformism.

Nor was the eccentricity of the scholar an end in itself. No doubt such a man – and it was often a man, though occasionally a woman, such as the Cambridge philosopher, Elizabeth Anscombe, a cigar-smoking mother of eight, who wore a monocle – provided moments of frustration for spouses, and for university administrators! But the Campbells and the Spooners and the Anscombes were not simply eccentrics: they were *academic* eccentrics; that is, their oddness was, first and foremost, of the *mind*, which translated comprehensively into the rest of their lives, most conspicuously their dress and demeanor. They were often impressive scholars and writers and teachers. Their eccentricity was the expression of a distinctive culture, a culture of curiosity, of absorption in learning – and learning that was self-propelled, not dictated by university committees or government bureaus or corporate entities. In the words of Samuel Johnson, "curiosity is, in great and generous minds, the first passion and the last; and perhaps always predominates in proportion to the strength of the contemplative faculties."[9] The seeming remoteness of scholars, their lack of social normality and conformity, has at once reflected and reinforced a spirit of intellectual detachment. There is indeed something unworldly about the academic eccentric, which has helped to detach the scholar from the obsessive fashions and absorptions of an over-organised society, and protect a perspective of objectivity.

Unfortunately, this over-organisation now threatens to engulf academic life. It militates against the life of an independent scholar within universities, making far less likely the presence, and even the survival, of the academic eccentric. Various factors have registered an impact in the midst of this over-organisation, either contributing

---

[9] Samuel Johnson, *Rambler* #150 (24 August 1751).

to it or flowing from it; factors which have made the present-day university less hospitable to genuine scholarship, and cast doubt on the university's educational condition and value in the current institutional form.

These factors fall into two broad categories. Some are practical and organisational, affecting the university as an institution. Others are intellectual and cultural – and, I believe, spiritual, at their core – relating to what has happened to the academic mind and intellectual culture. Together I think they have conspired to erode confidence in the university as a centre of learning in our society. This development is rendered even more serious by the extent to which the world of learning has come to be, as mentioned earlier, almost entirely absorbed by the university, so that learning itself is now deeply institutionalised, and subject to cultural and political pressures and sanctions that have crucial implications for the world of culture as well as of learning. Universities seem no longer aware of the extent to which they need independent scholars, and rely on the scholarly energy and insight outside of their walls to sustain a life of learning.

The first practical change to be highlighted is the clash of cultures that has taken place in universities in recent decades. This has arisen from the penetration of a scholarly culture by an alien culture, a culture of managerial supervision and accountability that dwells on structures and means, insisting on a uniformity of approach and the imposition of tests that are based, not on scholarly criteria and the search for truth and wisdom, but on the bureaucratic measurement of processes, the designated aim of which is compliance, even when it is disguised by the invoking of words such as "quality," as in "quality audit" and "quality assurance."

No doubt the university as an institution has always been subject to market and managerial influences, as in the Middle Ages when it was preparing people especially for ecclesiastical office;

or, in the age of colonial expansion, for imperial leadership and service. The difference now is that the actual life of learning has become invaded, so that learning itself is thought to be dubious and indefensible without vocational direction or political regulation and manipulation. The politics of bureaucratic surveillance are supplanting the culture of intellectual appetite and scholarly responsibility.

A second practical change is the massive expansion of higher education in Australia in recent decades. This has intensified pressure, both time and teaching pressure, on academic staff, and reduced the capacity, not only for research but, at a more fundamental level, for thinking, so that the mental space for independent scholarship, and the leisure to carry it out – leisure, in the classical and medieval sense of a condition of intellectual freedom and reflection, rather than of utilitarian relaxation[10] – have been greatly lessened. The expansion of universities has led to a proliferation of courses and degrees, which reflects both the intense specialisation of academic life and the claims of vocational preparation, and produced a narrowing of intellectual focus that detracts from the breadth and integration of understanding that should characterise the scholar.

The main justification for mass education at the university level in Australia has been utilitarian, a necessary form of employment preparation and income potential. It has not been connected, in any articulated way, to a higher or wider purpose, such as to prepare people for citizenship and democratic participation, or to heighten the intellectual and cultural benefits of learning. Yet the assumptions governing employment and income prospects arising from a university education are now coming under scrutiny as the

---

[10] See Josef Pieper, *Leisure: The Basis of Culture*, Pantheon Books, 1952, which treats of leisure as an attitude of mind and a condition of the soul that fosters a capacity to perceive reality.

link between a university degree and the earning of an attractive income is no longer assured. Prior to the May 2017 Federal Budget, which foreshadowed a higher student share of university fees, there was debate about the growing rate of unemployment among graduates. A workforce economist, Ian Li from the University of Western Australia, commented:

> The graduate degree premium has been eroding for some time. Private returns to higher education are still positive but they are no longer what they once were.[11]

If these doubts grow, the mass popularity of universities may decline. We may begin, as a society, to question the social status of a university degree and the idea that universities are good for everyone. While the prospect of universal higher education, complementing education at the primary and secondary levels, might be flattering to egalitarian sensibilities and yearnings, it reflects the mistake that treating people equally has come to mean treating them identically. (I speak as the father of a plumber as well as the father of a university lecturer.)

At the same time, it is important to recognise that a society needs well-formed elites, especially spiritual and intellectual elites, in order to cultivate qualities of vision and leadership and sustain the popular understanding and confidence necessary for the life of a culture. The poet James McAuley stressed this need in 1976, shortly before he died:

> All societies depend on the presence of elites, which are – with whatever failures, limitations and delinquencies natural to the human condition – bodies of people with superior discipline, capability of responsibility and leadership, sources of morale and integrity.[12]

---

[11] *The Australian*, 29-30 April 2017, 1.
[12] James McAuley, "A Small Testament," *Quadrant*, Vol. 20, No. 12, Decem-

The formation of elites, as McAuley noted, hinges on the influence of home and school rooted in tradition. He identified four matrices in Australia in which elites have been traditionally nurtured – three of them of religious origin (Anglican, non-conformist/ evangelical, and Catholic) and the fourth from the humanist-rationalist tradition.[13] These matrices, serving as fonts of intellectual insight, moral integrity, and cultural and political leadership, were also fundamental to the production of scholars, and especially independent scholars, for it gave them, not only the inspiration for intellectual work, but also the discipline and desire to serve wider communities.

Christopher Dawson was conscious of the historical significance of a spiritual elite, the priesthood, and how it functioned in various societies as a culture-building institution. The priesthood had an intellectual foundation. It constituted a learned class that had mastered a body of knowledge, and it provided the historical cradle for the intellectual elites of secular modernity. It had a stabilising influence on societies by its preservation of sacred rituals, which gave regular opportunities for the enactments of our spiritual nature in a material world; the saving of the world, as Christ's Incarnation attested, by means of the stuff of the world.

Modern secular society shuts out any religiously inspired office, and would recognise no connection – in fact, only an antipathy – between learning and religious faith; but it finally has to reckon with the consequences of such an exclusion. The price of banning religious elites, with a different philosophy and scale of values from that of secular elites, is to open up a vast social and political void that has immense implications for individual health and cultural integrity. This is what happens with the slaying of a transcendental vision and value system.

---

ber 1976, 10.
[13] Ibid.

Chesterton once said that poets are "those who rise above the people by understanding them."[14] An intellectual elite needs to be of the same disposition. This does not suggest, should not suggest, social superiority or political dominance (though we know these are not easy to avoid). It certainly should not imply superior behaviour. It suggests, rather, insight and sympathy, a profound affinity with the hungers and needs of ordinary people, and a capacity to capture these in the forms of the culture – its social institutions and laws and moral values, as well as its imaginative expressions, such as symbols and rituals, poetry, art and music. This capacity should be enhanced by the scholar's freedom from institutional pressures, not only to bow to embedded elitist opinion, but also to "publish or perish," which imposes on scholars an imperative to write and speak continually, even when they might have little or nothing to say.

A final practical change affecting present-day universities is the pressures on scholarly publication, which are beginning to compromise its integrity and credibility. One form of pressure arises from the growth of electronic publishing as increasingly the main channel by which scholarly findings are reported. Traditional print publications, both books and journals, involved considerable time and production processes, which had the unintended effect of enforcing delays and providing inbuilt opportunities for review and safeguards of quality. By contrast, the electronic world allows anyone to publish anything, and to distribute it immediately, at times more quickly than might have been planned as a result of hitting the Send button on the computer prematurely. At the high end of electronic publishing, these risks can be managed by pay walls and password access, but the intrinsic nature of the medium tends to impose a regime of haste that makes quality control more difficult.

---

[14] G.K. Chesterton, "The Three Kinds of Men," *Alarms and Discursions*, Methuen, 1927, 149.

On the positive side, however, the very ease and cheapness of electronic facilities represents a new advantage for the independent scholar. The electronic revolution has ushered in an era of self-publishing, and afforded a new freedom and flexibility in communication. While economic factors account for the demise of the traditional independent scholar – in that it is no longer financially viable for a person to pursue such a vocation without the support of an institution or, more rarely, a patron (such as the late Bill Leak enjoyed in the early years of his artistic and cartooning career) – the countervailing factor of personal communication, based on such devices as the iPhone and the iPad, has given scholars a degree of independence from institutions, and perhaps especially libraries, that was unimaginable a few decades ago. These conditions are proving vital for the many independent scholars who may be pre- or ex-academics, such as displaced PhD graduates unable to secure university employment, or retired academics, who can access various channels of online enquiry and communication, via blogs and other means, and disseminate research findings as well as scholarly (and even, at times, not so scholarly) opinion.

A second issue touching quality control is editorial and peer review, a mechanism that has traditionally ensured the dependability of scholarly publications. This is no longer as certain as it once was. There is an increasing incidence of corruption of the system, demonstrated by flawed research papers of various kinds, involving fabrication of data and of peer reviews, doctoring of images, and the citing of imaginary editorial boards. In early 2017, a UK parliamentary enquiry into the integrity of university research heard evidence of increasing scientific misconduct, which has given rise to a growing number of corrections and retractions.[15]

---

[15] See, for example, the reports of Kylar Loussikian in *The Australian*, 4 May 2016, and 25 May 2016, and an editorial on scientific publishing, "Breaking Free," in *The Economist*, 25 March 2017.

In addition to the practical changes to universities and academic culture, which have implications for the independent scholar, there are institutional and cultural developments that are limiting and distorting intellectual independence.

One is the politicisation of the university, notably in academic programs in the fashionable areas of the humanities and social sciences that have become infected by identity politics. There is, among at least a vocal proportion of academic staff, a tight uniformity of political attitudes – a form of compliance, one might say – essentially of the cultural Left, which is hostile to the traditions and values of Western civilisation, stigmatising them as backward and oppressive. Universities have become constrained by an ideological straitjacket, which favours advocacy over the contest of ideas, and raises serious issues about their reputation for academic freedom.

A second development is the rising atmosphere of intimidation, mob-based and media-promoted, at times physically threatening, which has led to a new generation of campus protests.[16] This is especially so in America, but it is now emerging in Australia as well, as was shown in 2015 at Sydney University when a visiting pro-Israeli speaker was interrupted by a violent protest led by the Director of the University's Centre for Peace and Conflict Studies.

In the light of my own memory, conditioned by the campus protests of the 1960s, the present era seems rather restrained. The difference now, however, is that the rise of identity politics among intellectual and media elites reflects a new form of intellectual conditioning that is taking root in universities and elsewhere. It is

---

[16] Stephen M. Krason, "On a New Generation of Campus Disorders," *Crisis Magazine*, 2 December 2015, and Stanley Kurtz, "Understanding the Campus Free-Speech Crisis," *National Review Online*, 12 April 2017; and reports on college protests and campus free speech in *The Economist*, 11 March 2017, 33, and 1 April 2017, 31.

not easy to hope for a recovery of what the Australian poet Vincent Buckley once called the "great tradition of intellectual chivalry"[17] in Western culture. The approach now being adopted is a new version of Voltairean wisdom, once wryly expressed by Ronald Reagan, that modern liberals will "defend to the death your right to agree with them."[18]

Among present-day ironies, the old liberal value of free speech is now falling to conservatives to defend. While liberals lurch towards totalitarian controls, as though moral meaning can be legally imposed rather than drawn from transcendental sources, conservatives embrace a libertarian autonomy, relying on self-chosen identities at odds with a broad sense of community. Both these quests represent bleak prospects for Western society, and in pursuit of them we suffer from an extraordinary readiness to being offended; in fact, the "offence industry" may be responsible, in a perverse way, for a new form of "manufacturing" in Australia and other Western countries. As one Canadian journalist has commented:

> In the new order, a high level of suggestibility and a low
> level of common sense will be important survival skills.[19]

A more subtle – and insidious – form of intellectual conditioning now taking place is the notion of collective guilt, which is giving rise not only to apologies for the behaviour of our ancestors, but to the removal of any signs of their historical existence, such as changing the commemorative names of buildings in universities or public places. The aim is to rewrite history so that it is "cleansed," free of all signs of what are now seen as objectionable biases. James

---

[17] Sir Arnold Lunn, *Unkilled for So Long*, Allen & Unwin, 1968, 108.
[18] Steven F. Hayward, *Greatness: Reagan, Churchill and the making of Extraordinary Leaders*, Crown Publishing, 2005, ch. 6.
[19] Denyse O'Leary, "The War on Freedom Is Rotting Our Intellectual Life," www.mercator.com, 2 May 2017, 4.

V. Schall has argued that the desire to take on collective guilt – for a past in which we personally played no part – is to impose the norms of one generation on another. It is being used to justify punishing those who are long dead, whom we can no longer personally accuse or arrest or put on trial – nor, of course, are they in a position to defend themselves. Schall asks: "How far back do we pursue our cleansing vengeance?"[20]

To return to Sir John Squire, who was, in addition to being an independent scholar and an eccentric, a cricket "tragic." He formed a team, aptly called The Invalids, which played occasional village games. Their cricketing performances, so quintessentially English, are immortalised in the social satire by A.G. Macdonell, called *England, Their England* (1933), which includes a caricature of Sir John Squire. In one Invalids game, Squire's side was fielding and the batsman at the crease skied a ball. Squire screamed out: "Leave it to Carstairs." The ball rose in the sky and eventually came down, with a heavy thud on the grass. No one caught it. Squire then realised – Carstairs had died the year before!

We know that we cannot "leave it to Carstairs"! The independent scholar lives a life of relative isolation, but his survival is likely to depend on some measure of community and solidarity – with other scholars, and with intellectually sympathetic institutions and organisations; both in person and with electronic assistance. I am greatly heartened by the presence in Australia of the Christopher Dawson Centre in Hobart, and of Campion College in Sydney, for they offer a spiritual and intellectual home to independent scholarship and learning. As Dawson himself recognised as an historical reality:

[E]very advance in education has been prepared by a pre-

---

[20] James V. Schall SJ, "On Collective Guilt," www.thecatholicthing.org, 9 May 2017.

liminary period in which the pioneers work outside the recognised academic cadres. This was so at the beginning of the European university and in the beginnings of humanism, while today the diffusion of leisure throughout the affluent society offers new opportunities for free intellectual activity.[21]

At the same time, Dawson realised the importance of individual friendships and support. "Conversation is more than bread and meat to me," he once confided to a friend. "I cannot exist without it."[22]

Karl Marx, that well-known independent scholar, put it well – or almost did when rallying the proletariat to release themselves from their chains. With apologies to BBC Radio's Frank Muir and Denis Norden, Karl Marx went so close to saying: "Working scholars of the world, unite. You have nothing to lose but your brains!"

[21] Christopher Dawson, *The Crisis of Western Education*, Sheed & Ward, 1961, 155-156.
[22] Magdalen Goffin, *The Watkin Path: An Approach to Belief – The Life of E.I. Watkin*, Sussex Academic Press, 2006, 129.

# 9

# KNOWLEDGE WITHOUT WISDOM[1]

## *Steven Schwartz*

Macquarie University in Sydney is a big place, and sometimes visitors get lost. To help people navigate their way around, the university distributed maps at strategic locations around the campus. One day some graffiti appeared on one of the maps. Under the orientation arrow, the one that says, "You are here", someone had added, "but why?" Not a bad question. Why do universities exist? What, exactly, is the purpose of higher education or any education for that matter? Our search for an answer to these questions begins in an unlikely place, London's Gatwick airport.

### Knowledge is not wisdom

Julie Lloyd was 59 years old and was returning to Canada after a visit to England. With her greying hair and warm smile, she looked like a kindly grandmother. But looks, as they say, can be deceiving. To the ever-alert security staff at London's Gatwick airport, Julie was a potential terrorist who brazenly tried to smuggle a gun aboard a flight from London to Toronto.

Perhaps "smuggle" is too strong a word. Julie didn't try to conceal the weapon; it was in the handbag she submitted for airport scanning. "Gun" is also not entirely accurate. The item in question was 6-cm long, and it was attached to the hands of a small plastic soldier. Julie had bought the toy soldier for her husband, a former

---

[1] Parts of this chapter appeared in different form in the *Times Higher Education Supplement, The Australian,* and the *Australian Literary Review.*

army signaller, but the Gatwick security staff would not let her carry in on board. Julie protested strenuously. "The 'gun', she said, is made of resin, it has no moving parts. There is no hole in the barrel; there isn't even a trigger". Of course, the security staff could see all this for themselves. Nevertheless, they insisted that the tiny toy was a prohibited "firearm" and they prevented Julie from taking it aboard the plane.

When Julie arrived in Toronto, she complained to her friends back in England. They took the story to the tabloid *Daily Mail* newspaper (the largest circulation newspaper in the UK). The editor sent a journalist to interview the head of security at Gatwick Airport. The head of security agreed that the story sounds "incredibly stupid", but he explained that "rules are rules and we must obey".

I had my own encounter with the "rules are rules" argument when I visited the Sydney office of Medibank Private after an extended stay abroad. I explained that I had been living overseas for some years, but I had now returned home and wanted to re-activate my health insurance. "No problem", said the person behind the desk. "All we need is proof that you have returned to Australia". I was not sure how to respond. I decided to try logic. "Well", I said, "this office is in Sydney, Sydney is in Australia, and I'm sitting here right in front of you. Does this not provide sufficient evidence for you to infer that I am in Australia?" "Not really," she said, "I need documentary proof". I offered to let her pinch me, but the lady was not for turning. Until she saw an arrival stamp in my passport (something Australian immigration has not done for years), or a boarding pass, or a luggage tag, there would be no health insurance for me.

It is true that Julie's story and my encounter with bureaucracy are only minor irritants, risible tales that cause little real harm. But, this is not always the case. Sometimes, rule following can lead to serious consequences.

A few years ago a teenage boy on a hike became lost in the re-mote bush outside of Sydney. Exhausted and dehydrated, he was still able to ring the emergency number using his mobile phone. The boy pleaded with the operator to send someone to rescue him. Alas, the service rules specified a particular requirement; the caller had to provide an address or at least the name of the nearest cross street. The boy was in the bush, in the Blue Mountains, well off the beaten track. There were no cross streets; in fact, there were no streets of any kind. But the operator was adamant – no street, no help. Help was delayed, and by the time the boy was found, it was too late. He was dead. The boy may have died anyway, but hidebound adherence to a rule turned a dangerous situation into a deadly one.

At the subsequent inquest, the emergency services manager agreed that the operators seemed "fixated" on obtaining a street address, but the manager defended them because they were only doing what they were trained to do. The manager may not have realised it, but the case highlighted one of the oldest controversies in teaching – the difference between training and education, between acquiring technical knowledge and becoming wise. The airport security staff who refused to distinguish a toy gun from a real one, the health insurance clerk who would not accept my corporeal presence as evidence that I was indeed in Australia, and the emergency call centre operators who asked a boy lost in the bush for a street address had all been carefully trained. They knew the protocols, understood the systems, and stuck to the rules. They had the necessary knowledge; what they lacked was the wisdom to apply it.

We frequently hear about a so-called "skills" shortage; suppos-edly there are too few plumbers or computer scientists or personal trainers. We must increase the skill level of our working population so that we can compete in the knowledge economy. (Is there some-where an economy based on ignorance?) Unfortunately, it is not enough to train people to follow a set of rules. Real-world problems are rarely cut and dry; they are often ambiguous and ill defined. They are not always covered in training because it is impossible to anticipate every contingency. A wise person knows how to improvise and when to make an exception to the rules.

## Wisdom has disappeared from campus

Unfortunately, wisdom has an image problem. As far as the popular media are concerned, wisdom is the province of ghost whisperers, extraterrestrials – think Mr. Spock the Vulcan – and wizened kung-fu sages ("The body is the arrow, the spirit is the bow, Grasshopper"). Wise people are not only portrayed as old, alien and weird but also bookish, risk-averse and unemotional. No wonder their pearls of wisdom are routinely ignored by the impetuous young. Youth thirsts for new experiences; it's in the nature of young people to take chances and follow their hearts. Wisdom just gets in the way. "Fools rush in where wise men never go", says the old song, "But wise men never fall in love, so how are they to know?"

You might think that universities would hold a different view; after all, they are in the wisdom business. You might think this, but you would be wrong. University courses cover every conceivable area of knowledge – massage therapy, homeopathy, circus performing – but "wisdom" is rarely mentioned.

It was not always like this. Wisdom, at least a religious version of wisdom, was central to the university for centuries, and its importance persisted right down to John Henry Newman's day. But wisdom is no longer on the curriculum. Distressed by its disappearance, academics have responded in their usual way – by writing books. In the last few years, they have published a plethora of worthy tomes, each lamenting the decline of higher education. There are now so many such books that the decline of academia has become a literary genre all its own. No doubt Amazon will soon offer an end-of-the-university-as-we-know-it box set (available as e-books, no doubt).

The authors of these books chart the symptoms of decay: more and more vocational courses; fewer and fewer humanities courses; and generations of students leaving university no wiser than the day they entered. The *leitmotif* of the academic declinism literature is money – sometimes too little, and sometimes too much. In his book, *Universities in the Market Place,*[2] former Harvard President Derek Bok talks about the problems of too much money. He argues that "excessive commercialisation in every part of the university" has corrupted traditional academic values. For example, when the free exchange of information – a bedrock virtue of academia – collides with the secrecy requirements of patents and profit making, it is the latter that always win. Bok also decries the conflicts of interest that arise when academics become entrepreneurs. For example, academics trying to commercialise a new drug have been known to suppress research findings that fail to support the drug's efficacy.

David Kirp, the author of *Shakespeare, Einstein and the Bottom Line,*[3] notes that the impetus to make money has elevated subjects that have immediate financial returns (like commerce for example) over less bankable ones such as the humanities. In *Saving Higher Education in the Age of Money,*[4] James Engell and Anthony Dangerfield claim that we have inverted the traditional role of money in universities. Students and their families no longer shop around for the best education that "money can buy". Instead, they seek the education that will "buy the most money".

Education wasn't always about money. From its ancient

---

[2] Derek Bok (2004). *Universities in the marketplace.* Princeton, NJ: Princeton University Press.

[3] David Kirp (2004). *Shakespeare, Einstein and the bottom line: the marketing of higher education.* Cambridge, MA: Harvard University Press.

[4] James Engell and Anthony Dangerfield (2005). *Saving higher education in the age of money.* Charlottesville, VA: University of Virginia Press.

origins until recently, academics defined their mission in moral terms. Following Plato, they believed that education makes good people, and good people act nobly. In the last century, the decline in religion and the widespread acceptance of moral relativism, even idiot nihilism, forced universities to abandon their traditional moral aims – building character, inculcating ethical values, and transmitting culture.

Having lost their time-honoured purposes universities looked for a replacement. Not surprisingly, the one they found reflects the primary concern of modern society – making money. Vice chancellors pay economists to produce reports showing how much their institutions contribute to the national accounts. Indeed, universities put so much emphasis on their financial benefits that our politicians came to believe that they exist for no other reason. The result is that we are now firmly in the age of money in which the value of higher education is measured by how much money graduates earn for themselves and the country. Research, once motivated by the desire to understand ourselves and our place in the universe, is now measured by its "impact". Subjects that focus on self-understanding are marginalised in favour of disciplines that can be easily translated into cash.

Supporters of the humanities defend themselves by arguing that impact is not limited to the sciences, engineering, and medicine – the humanities make money too. Take Shakespeare, for example. The Bard is the epitome of a "creative industry". Tourists flock to Stratford-upon-Avon spending their money in the local hotels, bars, and souvenir shops. Large audiences are attracted to Shakespeare's plays. Copies of his sonnets continue to bring in millions, and even the wine sold during the interval at the Globe theatre earns lots of money

All true. There is only one problem. Shakespeare's true value has nothing to do with any of this. I know it has been said before but it bears repeating, we seem to know the price of everything and the value of nothing. Don't get me wrong. I am not against getting rich. As screen siren Mae West once said: "I've been rich and I've been poor and, believe me, rich is better." As a former vice chancellor, I know as well as anyone that money is the means by which universities achieve their goals. ("As our Parish priest used to reply when asked why the church always needs more money, "No margin, no mission".) But surely the first step is to have a mission. Otherwise, universities become institutions with means but no ends.

## The mission of the university

What should the mission of a university be? In *Not for Profit: Why Democracy Needs the Humanities*,[5] Martha Nussbaum argues that the mission of a university is, or should be, to prepare students for democratic citizenship. Democracy makes severe demands on it citizens. Rather than simply defer to authority, citizens in a democracy need to know how to weigh the relevant evidence for themselves. Before they can form a view about the important issues of the day, citizens must be able to reflect on social issues and translate their knowledge and values into a defensible policy position.

If done correctly – using logic and relying on evidence – the opportunity to argue and debate enhances mutual respect and understanding. Students learn that those who hold different views from theirs are not necessarily evil or stupid. Indeed, Nussbaum considers developing empathy to be one of the most important goals of higher education. Seeing the world through others' eyes, envisaging distant times and remote places are part of what Nussbaum calls the "sympathetic imagination"– the frame of mind that allows us to feel in touch with "lives at a distance".

---

[5] Martha Nussbaum (2010). *Not for profit: why democracy needs the humanities.* Princeton, NJ: Princeton University Press.

By aiming for skills rather than wisdom, Nussbaum believes that higher education has become trivialised. Anthony Kronman agrees. In his book, *Education's End: Why Our Colleges and Universities Have Given up on the Meaning of Life*,[6] Kronman alleges that the humanities have lost their way, at least in part, because they have been trying to emulate the sciences, seeking objective facts and aspiring to "value-free knowledge".

Kronman blames this on a combination of political correctness and postmodernism that has made academics wary of judging some books, thoughts, and ideas to be more important or even, God forbid, better than others. Yet, as citizens in a democracy, graduates will be required to make many judgements, on juries, for example, and every time they vote. A good education does not tell students what judgement to make; it teaches them how to gather relevant facts, analyse arguments, and reach conclusions.

Kronman goes one step further. He believes that universities should help students find meaning in their lives. His prescription for this is the careful reading of the great works of philosophy and literature. (Of course, only the congenitally foolhardy would try to produce a list of such must-read books, which I once did. I will not go into this here.)

**Lost souls**

In a supposedly secular age, souls loom unexpectedly large in the literature of academic declinism. *The Lost Soul of Higher Education*[7] by Ellen Schrecker and Harry R. Lewis's *Excellence Without a Soul*[8] are two examples. I do not think I have ever heard a single

---

[6] Anthony Kronman (2007). *Education's end: why our colleges and universities have given up on the meaning of life.* New Haven, CT: Yale University Press.

[7] Ellen Schrecker (2010). *The Lost Soul of Higher Education.* New York, NY: The New Press.

[8] Harry R. Lewis (2006). *Excellence without a Soul.* New York, NY: Public Affairs.

academic utter the word soul, at least not in connection with university learning. Yet soul is exactly the right word. Our universities have made a Faustian bargain. Like the scholar in Goethe's play, they have traded away their souls, and such transactions rarely turn out to be win-win propositions.

Today's universities are mainly concerned with preparing students for a career. There is nothing wrong with vocational training; a fulfilling career is an important part of a good life. But, while we are teaching students the state of their particular art, we must also be concerned with the state of their hearts. To paraphrase John Ruskin, the highest reward for a university education is not what graduates get for it but what they become by it. Yes, we must prepare graduates for what they will *do,* but we also have a duty to help them to at least think about what kind of people they want to *be*. Indeed, these two educational goals are inextricable.

No one would try to argue that a deep knowledge of philosophy makes surgeons better at removing a prostate. But it might deepen their empathy and improve their understanding of what constitutes a high-quality life, both of which could help them to decide whether they should remove a prostate in the first place.

Of course, it is not just doctors who could benefit from a broader education. Studying drama would not have helped financiers devise the complicated financial derivatives that plunged the world into financial crisis, but if they were familiar with *Faust*, they might have thought twice about the consequences of their actions. Being able to quote Shelley will not help politicians get elected (certainly not in Australia) but studying *Ozymandias* might make them more humble and thoughtful about their accomplishments.

Perhaps I have gone too far. A generation of graduates familiar with the great works of history, philosophy, and literature is a worthy vision, but reading widely does not guarantee wisdom.

Reading, by itself, will not make anyone wise. Experience is also required. As Odysseus learns on his journey back to Ithaca, some lessons can only be learned the hard way – through experience. Nothing has changed. Youth start out with sex, drugs and rock and roll and with experience they eventually come to appreciate the Delphic prescription "nothing to excess".

There is a problem, however. Experience, alone, cannot guarantee wisdom any more than reading can. The lessons of life are only available to those who are ready to learn them. Pasteur famously said that "Chance favours the prepared mind", and university academics should take his words seriously.

What really matters?

Universities need to go beyond vocational training. Life, death, love, beauty, courage, loyalty – we have stripped all of these from our modern curricula. Still, when it comes time to sum up our lives, they are the only things that ever really matter to anyone. Each year on Ash Wednesday, the priest admonishes the faithful to "remember, that thou art dust, and to dust thou shalt return." A salutary reminder of what we all have waiting for us. In the meantime, like the Preacher in *Ecclesiastes,* we spend our years trying to find some meaning in our lives.

It is easy to fall into the pit of nihilism, to consider life "a tale told by an idiot, full of sound and fury, signifying nothing". But before we let our students reach this conclusion, we should at least try to provide them with the intellectual foundation they need to make such a judgement.

In *Choruses from The Rock,*[9] T. S. Eliot asks: "Where is the wisdom we have lost in knowledge? Where is the knowledge we have lost in information?" Knowledge and information are not enough. The security guards at Gatwick, the health insurance agent

---

[9] T.S. Eliot (1973). *Choruses from the rock*. London: Faber and Faber.

in Sydney and the emergency operators who insisted on having a street name before they could respond all knew the required procedure. They probably also had the moral will to do the right thing. What they lacked was moral skill – they lacked wisdom. Without wisdom, knowledge and information are useless, perhaps even dangerous.

Mahatma Gandhi knew this. He warned us to be on guard against science without humanity, politics without principle, knowledge without character, wealth without work, commerce without morality, pleasure without conscience, and worship without sacrifice.

It is not easy for universities to go against the utilitarian flow but it is our duty to try. As author Flannery O'Connor wrote in a letter to a friend, "You have to push as hard as the age that pushes against you". It's time to bring "wisdom" back to campus.

# 10

## How the Arts Lost the Culture War

*John Simons*

For a couple of years now there has been an increasing promotion of the skill of coding. It is claimed that coding will be the key employability skill of the next decade. This may or may not be true: predicting trends in the labour market when the successive tidal waves of digitisation, globalisation and robotisation have yet fully to hit the beach is a very risky business. But it is also claimed that that coding has other, less instrumental, benefits. Inter alia, it is claimed that coding teaches logical thinking and good discipline in mental organisation. It expands the cortex.

This campaign is interesting for a number of reasons.

The first is that whether or not it is true that coders will be in high demand in the future it would appear that these jobs are unlikely to be of high value and the majority of new employees will be tweaking apps for small businesses. The claim also ignores the probability that if thousands of coders really are needed the nature of the work is amply fitted to global outsourcing and the cheap labour markets of Asia are much more likely to benefit than the high cost ones of the Anglosphere and especially Australia. So the claim would appear – given that the need for highly skilled coders as opposed to jobbing techies is always going to be limited – to be largely about low level skilled work (and there is nothing wrong with that) and not, as it sometimes appears, the harbinger of a whole new profession with all the accoutrements of privilege and value that go with that. The reality is much more likely to be that hundreds of Australian children will be forced to spend much of their education learning a useless skill linked to an obsolete technology that will, if it leads to employment at all, lead only to drudgery. And sadly, but predictably, all this waste of time and spirit will be subsidised by government which is already showing piqued interest at a new and shiny toy. But luckily the taxpayer is there to fund it all.

The second reason that the coding vogue should claim our attention is that while the claims made for the more general intellectual benefits of learning coding may be true (although similar things could be said about doing hard Sudoku or cryptic crosswords or learning the street map of London) these claims could validly be made for other educational options some of which might not only expand the cortex but also offer benefits for global citizenship. The most obvious of these is the chance to learn a foreign language and, indeed, almost every non-instrumental claim for the benefits of learning coding that I have seen could be made more strongly for learning a natural language. More strongly, not least because learning a language opens up communication channels with a globalised community as well as offering access to the culture and thought of other people.

The third reason that we should be interested in coding is that in spite of the undeniable truth of the claim that natural language learning offers all the benefits claimed for coding I have not detected any claim of this kind from the language education community and the reasons for this are worth brief exploration. There has been some stirring of interest in the science faculties of universities but this largely misses the point that the coding boom (if such there will be) will take place at a much lower level than is required to revive the flagging fortunes of academic information technology and that any adult wishing to learn to code will be much better off doing a cheap or free online course in his or her own time rather than submitting to the expensive and inflexible regime of a university. And the market will determine that they do just that so there is unlikely to be any real part for universities in this bonanza should it occur. Although interest from science faculties is understandable, as students mean money, the lack of response from the language departments of arts faculties is, on the face of it, less easy to comprehend as this would surely be a *casus belli* around which to organise a much needed campaign for the revival of language teaching and learning in Australia. I once heard a very eminent person lament his monolingualism. I once heard a group of senior arts academics lament that Australia is a monolingual country. This is as far from the truth as it is possible to get. What is, alas, largely true is that educated Australians are often monolingual. A combination of lack of opportunity and lack of will has prevented universities from addressing this and the largely inequitable processes by which many Australian universities go about recruiting their students (i.e. a reliance on the ATAR system which is little more than a proxy for economic opportunity and a post code map) have inhibited the mobilisation of the immense linguistic talent of the Australian public at large as an academic and cultural resource for the nation.

In contemplating the phenomenon of coding it occurred to me that the curious passivity of university language departments when the very arguments they require are being handed to them on a plate might be a symptom of a larger phenomenon which goes the heart of the purpose of universities in general and the role of liberal education in particular. The remainder of this brief paper will be spent exploring that thought.

To understand the problem we need to start by considering a number of things: changes in the perceived role of universities over the last thirty years or so; the motivations of students for going to university at all; the internal dynamic of universities especially regarding the allocation of costs and approaches to income; the incentives and disincentives which drive individual academics.

Broadly speaking, Australian and British universities have followed similar paths since the 1980s. An expansion of university places and changes in the funding model to increase the contribution of the students have accompanied a societal shift by which going to university is a much more common experience than ever before. This also means that universities have moved from being politically neutral ground to a point where there might be votes to be won and lost in higher education policy. This change has not gone unnoticed in the Parliament although I do not think that its implications (especially for transparency and public accountability) have yet been fully understood in universities.

The expansion of universities was largely carried out in what might most kindly be called a policy neutral environment in which the vaguest assumptions of the generic benefit of higher education, if not for all at least for the many, were deployed (and there are some merits in some of these views) and universities were given autonomy to work out how to implement the change. What this meant was that most of them – the vast majority – did not consider how a student body much changed in both scale and character might require shifts not only in approaches to teaching but also in curriculum and outcomes. Rather they tried to carry on as before while making allowances for bigger classes and bigger calls on the physical infrastructure and consumable resource base. The inefficient models that emerged inevitably reduced the relative value of funding per student. The universities called this process 'government cuts'. But universities cannot be blamed for this. Indeed, given the rapidity of change they faced it would have been hard for them to do much else. However, thirty or so years on the impact of this is being felt in unsustainable business models which will, I believe, soon begin to collapse, especially as the sectoral response to globalisation and digitisation has similarly lacked imagination and proactivity. To put it bluntly universities are now in a vice where the forces of the past and those of the future are combining to squeeze them to death and the profound conservatism and myopic self interest of their professional culture means that they are quite unable to do anything about it.

However, if governments were happy to pass off to universities the responsibility for making sense of the changes they were promoting and universities were happy to do that by minimising the idea of change the same could not be said of the new generations of students and the taxpayers who would fund them. It appears that they were more than able to fill in the policy blanks and make their own decisions about what the benefits of going to university might be. And these benefits were seen not so much as about the intangible pleasures of liberal or technical education but about the much more instrumental joys of better jobs and higher salaries. In a word: employability.

Now, there is nothing new in the proposition that people go to university in order to improve their job prospects. In my own undergraduate days where only about 2% of my peer group went to university most people who were not training for a profession believed, with justification, that they would get a good job at the end of their studies. And hardly any of them believed that graduating in, say, history would mean that they would become historians.

So what has changed?

In the first place, the relatively few graduates coming onto the job market in, say, 1978 were easily absorbed into 'graduate' jobs. In the second, the demography of the cohort meant that expectations about the relationship between what you studied and what you ended up doing were far less instrumental. In the third, the landscape of employment in those days meant that you could get very good jobs in business, manufacturing, local government, the public service, media or the law without being a graduate and so the many bright young people who chose not to go to university or couldn't get in (we forget how selective universities were in those days) had many excellent options which they could begin to enjoy straight out of school. Now such options are few and far between. One effect of these things was that in the UK, for example, the most popular subject and the most difficult to get into a university to read was English Literature and getting a job as a lecturer in English in the late 70s meant competing in fields which characteristically included more than a hundred applicants. This is barely comprehensible today but it was the case. And, interestingly, the first decade or so of expansion in the UK system led to no significant shift in the demography of the student body when considered through the lens of social class. All that happened was that the 'middle class' students who previously didn't want or need degrees were soaked up and only then did some more serious social diversification begin. Just at that point the screws were turned on the contributions expected from the students and their families.

In case I am misunderstood, the idea that most people go to university to improve their prospects is a perfectly reasonable one and universities should take it seriously. However, the policy vacuum in which universities were expanded meant that the employability criterion came to the fore as an artifact of a consumerist approach to education rather than a thought-through re-imagination of the purpose of higher education in a post-industrial social democracy and this, combined with the requirement of more and more employment sectors for graduates, changed the nature of the university irrespective of whether those who managed or worked in universities knew it or not or liked it or not. So business schools boomed (stoked up by huge influxes of overseas students especially from China) and increasingly curriculum became devoted to the development of 'employability skills' (which universities understand very poorly) at the cost of locating value in the guided academic study of a discipline.

Currently more than 90% of students believe that they will be better off as graduates than not and the figures bear out that this belief is correct. Pretty much any Australian graduate (fine and performing arts students are the exception) makes a profit on the deal by which they trade off fees and opportunity costs for a degree which will get them a higher salary and, crucially, long periods of continuous employment over a working life. However, the integrity of this proposition is getting harder and harder to maintain. Taxpayers fund universities on the basis of foregoing services they might have enjoyed instead and might well have preferred. Currently a naïve belief in employability drives consensus on the perceived benefit at the microeconomic level. But as that benefit becomes more and more attenuated, then, sooner or later, universities will be asked some very hard questions. Especially if government or opposition – it scarcely matters which – come to view expanded universities and student debt as vote losers rather than vote winners and present them as bloated entities delivering little social value and presided over by a cohort of overpaid and unworldly executives. This is already starting to happen both in the UK and here.

What all this means is that the 'culture war' of the title of this paper is not so much one between art and science or about liberal education vs vocational training (although it has elements of both of these) as between the idea of a university as a place of disinterested study vs the idea of the university as the means to the end of employment. The vulgar question asked of a philosophy student –'what are you going to do with it? (which was rarely asked forty years ago because everyone knew that the answer was 'become a civil servant') is now asked not only by the students themselves and the parents who bankroll many of them but also by people within universities including academics and those, elected or unelected, who supervise and frame funding policy. Ultimately the culture war was fought to maintain the truth of the fallacious and often meretricious proposition that there is and should be a connection between the subject of a degree and an outcome or pathway in the 'real world' or 'world of work' as we please to call it nowadays.

And why were the arts especially on the losing side?

There is, of course, a glib answer to this question around concepts of basic utility. But actually it is relatively easy to show how the skills derived from the study of the humanities confer all the employability benefits of more technical subjects and probably more and any perusal of what employers say they would like from their graduates (as opposed to what universities, in spite of the mountains of research on this topic, persist in providing) would add weight to the claim. There will not be a 21st century Matthew Arnold I imagine but the fact does remain that a well-judged campaign in favour of the humanities and contextualised by contemporary concerns with employability might win enough hearts and minds to make a difference even at this stage and the arts could easily inhabit a valued space in the repurposed training university. Three years ago the Chief Scientist published a major report concerning the future of employment and the necessity of scientific skills in that future. However, the figures produced did not, in my opinion at least and I am not a statistician, confirm that there was a major gap between employment prospects for science graduates and those for graduates of other disciplines. Nor were the attributes identified as most associated with science (STEM) disciplines necessarily unique to those disciplines – indeed, most of them appeared equally likely to have been developed by students in the humanities and social sciences. In addition, although there was some triumphalism about this report in Science faculties it doesn't seem to have been noticed that the skills described in the report were not necessarily those to be acquired through a science degree and that it is doubtful that current provision for science in universities does, in fact, confer much employability-related benefit. This is partly because the 'best' science student is not seen as someone who will complete their degree successfully and then go on to get a good job but as someone who will go on to postgraduate study and contribute to the Faculty's research effort.

But this is all just commentary: as things stand so much in the current university system will be swept away that the catastrophe awaiting the arts will hardly be noticeable. And I stress that there is nothing intrinsically wrong with having a publicly funded university system designed to deliver economic benefit both individually and socially if that is what is required. However, lack of policy and plans means that the system is now unsustainable and increasingly unable to deliver those benefits in either the private or public dimension.

So why do the arts establishments in universities not speak out? To understand this we have to look at the internal dynamics of universities, their competitive context and the incentives offered to academics who wish to pursue successful careers. I insist that I do not believe that the passivity of the arts and humanities in the face of the challenges I have outlined is due to any hebetude on the part of well meaning and hard working academics but rather a function of rational behavior given the environment in which they find themselves.

It is sadly true that for many universities nowadays the effective teaching of undergraduates is a secondary or even tertiary business operation (behind research and fund raising) and for many academics a necessary evil (a phrase I've actually heard a very promising young scholar use and you don't need to have much

imagination to know where he would have picked it up). This
didn't use to be the case so what has happened? The answer is that
research has changed in status and, in doing so, not only deformed
the outlook of universities in regard to their responsibilities to
the young and not so young people who entrust them with vast
amounts of time and money but also, in the long term, crippled
their business models. Successive UK governments found it hard
to pull policy levers that would encourage universities to compete
or cooperate until they came up with the competitive assessment
of research and making research funding contingent on success in
what is, essentially, a handicap chase where the favourites romp
home every time. Universities which had, until then, maintained
a sulky indifference to the pleas of government to become more
efficient immediately began to carve each other up. Especially those
who knew they would be running with short odds. A medley of also
runs follow the field every five years or so expecting a different
result from an unchanged situation. A similar thing has happened in
Australia and although the funding algorithms are not yet in place
they certainly will be.

Apart from the fact that undergraduates – full members of the
Collegiate body who should be the most important people in any
university – are now reduced to client status (in some universities
they are called customers), what does this change mean?
Traditionally, research effort and research funding, both internal
and external, was clustered in science, engineering and medicine.
Universities were pleased to see work in the humanities and social
sciences as an adornment but it was not expected to be a significant
fund raiser (unless one landed a massive private endowment) nor
was it funded beyond subsistence internally. This has changed and
humanities research is not only expected to bring in significant
money but also it is generously funded internally. This leads to an
impossible squeeze as the available money for arts research simply

doesn't, no matter how successful the enterprise, match the funding needed to produce it at current levels. Result: misery.

For the individual academic this deformation has especially malign consequences. She or he must concentrate on research in order to get promotion or pass probation or get a job at all. So humanities academics are –rationally as I have said – spending much if not most of their time on an activity which loses their university money (in the sense that the outlay isn't recouped) and adds little, if any, value to the experience of their students (indeed, it diminishes it by diverting funds which might be otherwise spent on teaching, really smart approaches to digitally afforded learning or reducing the staff-student ratio). In this circumstance we cannot be surprised that we don't hear a strong and cogent voice raised for the arts. What is there to say?

I was recently at a symposium in an Australian university where an early career academic opined that universities should be the locations of speculative research. And she was quite right – we must defend non-utilitarian inquiry as having a value in itself. But what she had not considered I suspect is that there is no reason to fund such research and that someone who would like to see, say, a cure for cancer might prefer their tax dollars to be spent on that rather than on post modern cultural theory interesting though that may be. It now seems barely possible for young academics in particular to imagine a world in which their research could take place in the absence of grants or in which they might simply concentrate their efforts on really good teaching and curriculum development and let that drive their other scholarly endeavours. And those who can see such a world cannot thrive because the prizes of promotion will frequently be denied them.

And that, best beloved, is how the arts lost the culture war.